SO-BZR-335

# GUIDE TO THE AUTOMOBILE MECHANIC CERTIFICATION EXAMINATION

## James G. Hughes

Automotive Training Instructor, Rio Hondo College
Certified General Automobile Mechanic
Former Toyota National Service Training Instructor

RESTON PUBLISHING COMPANY, INC.   Reston, Virginia
*A Prentice-Hall Company*

Library of Congress Cataloging in Publication Data

Hughes, James G
    Guide to the automobile mechanic certification
examination.

    1.  Automobiles--Maintenance and repair--Examinations,
questions, etc.  I.  Title.
TL152.H858          629.28'7'22076             78-105
ISBN 0-8359-2618-4


ⓒ 1978 by
RESTON PUBLISHING COMPANY, INC., Reston, Virginia 22090
*A Prentice-Hall Company*

10   9   8   7

Printed in the United States of America.

# CONTENTS

# PREFACE

SOME BRIEF FACTS REGARDING THE AUTOMOBILE MECHANICS CERTIFICATION PROGRAM

NIASE (National Institute for Automotive Service Excellence) is a nonprofit corporation that has been organized to promote and encourage high standards of automobile service and repair. The Institute is governed by a 36-member Board of Directors. The members represent many different areas of the automotive service industry.

NIASE offers tests in eight specific areas of automobile repair. To become certified in a given repair area, you must pass that specific test. To become certified as a General Automobile Mechanic, you must pass all eight tests. The eight NIASE test areas are:

1. Engine Repair (80 questions)
2. Automatic Transmission (40 questions)
3. Manual Transmission and Rear Axle (40 questions)
4. Front End (40 questions)
5. Brakes (40 questions)
6. Electrical Systems (40 questions)
7. Heating and Air Conditioning (40 questions)
8. Engine Tune-up (80 questions)

NIASE also certifies in six areas of heavy-duty truck (and bus) repair, in body repair, and in painting and refinishing.

To take the test you must sign up in advance, and pay a $10.00 registration fee, plus $7.00 for each test you plan to take. To obtain a registration form, write to NIASE and request the free Bulletin of Information booklet. The address is:

National Institute for Automotive Service Excellence
1825 K Street, N.W.
Washington, D.C. 20006

Tests are conducted in about 250 cities across the nation, as indicated in the Bulletin of Information. The tests are given twice a year, once in the spring and once in the fall.

INSTRUCTIONS FOR USING THIS BOOK

This book contains eight sample pretests, one for each of the NIASE certification areas. Each pretest contains a large pool of realistic study questions. These questions are not taken from NIASE tests, but are similar in content and style to those you will find on actual certification tests. You should also be aware of the fact that the NIASE test questions are changed periodically.

The author recommends that you prepare for the NIASE tests by doing the following:

1. Find a quiet room where you won't be disturbed.

2. Decide which pretest you want to take.

3. Prepare yourself an answer sheet.

4. Take the pretest that you have selected, grade it using the answer key, and determine the areas you need to brush up on.

5. Start a study program using your own textbooks or those from a library. Refer to the study outline at the beginning of each pretest and the bibliography at the end of this book.

6. Check with your local schools for automotive training programs and any special refresher courses they may be scheduling.

These additional tips are made to the buyer of this book:

1. Read carefully the study outlines. Understand all of the terms, repair procedures, and diagnostic methods.

2. Be aware of the fact that on the actual NIASE tests there is a certain amount of question overlap. For instance, cooling system questions are asked on the Engine Repair test, the Engine Tune-up test, and the Heating and Air Conditioning test.

3. When studying for the Engine Repair test, refer also to the Engine Tune-up questions and the Electrical Systems questions.

4. When studying for the Engine Tune-up test, refer also to the Engine Repair questions and the Electrical Systems questions.

5. When you take the actual NIASE tests, an unanswered question counts as a wrong answer. If you are not sure of the correct answer, make the best guess you can.

6. When you take the actual NIASE test, read each question twice. The second time you may notice a key word that you overlooked the first time. Every word in the question is important and may be a clue to the right answer. Each question is of the multiple-choice type with four possible answers. Select the one that is most correct.

Following is a list of specific content areas contained in each NIASE test and what percent of the total questions are in each area.

BRAKES

| | |
|---|---|
| Hydraulic System Diagnosis and Repair | 28% |
| Drum Brake Diagnosis and Repair | 25% |
| Disc Brake Diagnosis and Repair | 30% |
| Power Assist Units Diagnosis and Repair | 5% |
| Miscellaneous Diagnosis and Repair | 12% |

FRONT END

| | |
|---|---|
| Steering Systems Diagnosis and Repair | 25% |
| Suspension Systems Diagnosis and Repair | 30% |
| Wheel Alignment Diagnosis, Adjustment and Repair | 30% |
| Wheel and Tire Diagnosis and Repair | 15% |

ENGINE REPAIR

| | |
|---|---|
| General Engine Diagnosis | 14% |
| Cylinder Head and Valve Train Diagnosis and Repair | 24% |
| Engine Block Diagnosis and Repair | 20% |
| Lubrication and Cooling Systems Diagnosis and Repair | 10% |
| Ignition System Diagnosis and Repair | 15% |
| Fuel and Exhaust Systems Diagnosis and Repair | 11% |
| Battery and Starting Systems Diagnosis and Repair | 6% |

ENGINE TUNE-UP

| | |
|---|---|
| General Engine Diagnosis | 20% |
| Ignition System Diagnosis and Repair | 21% |
| Fuel and Exhaust Systems Diagnosis and Repair | 15% |
| Emission Control Systems Diagnosis and Repair | 22% |
| Engine Related Service | 9% |
| Engine Electrical Systems Diagnosis and Repair | 13% |

## AUTOMATIC TRANSMISSIONS

| | |
|---|---|
| General Transmission Diagnosis | 30% |
| Transmission Maintenance and Adjustment | 10% |
| In-Car Transmission Repair | 25% |
| Off-Car Transmission Repair | 35% |

## MANUAL TRANSMISSION AND REAR AXLE

| | |
|---|---|
| Clutch Diagnosis and Repair | 18% |
| Transmission Diagnosis and Repair | 28% |
| Drive Shaft and Universal Joint Diagnosis and Repair | 12% |
| Rear Axle Diagnosis and Repair | 37% |
| Four Wheel Drive Diagnosis and Repair | 5% |

## ELECTRICAL SYSTEMS

| | |
|---|---|
| General Electrical System Diagnosis | 10% |
| Battery Diagnosis and Repair | 10% |
| Starting System Diagnosis and Repair | 15% |
| Charging System Diagnosis and Repair | 20% |
| Lighting Systems Diagnosis and Repair | 15% |
| Gauges and Warning Devices Diagnosis and Repair | 10% |
| Horn and Wiper/Washer Diagnosis and Repair | 8% |
| Accessories Diagnosis and Repair | 12% |

## HEATING AND AIR CONDITIONING

| | |
|---|---|
| A/C System Diagnosis and Repair | 22-28% |
| Refrigeration System Component Diagnosis and Repair | 32% |
| Heating and Engine Cooling Systems Diagnosis and Repair | 18-22% |
| Control Units Diagnosis and Repair | 22% |

# ACKNOWLEDGEMENTS

Specific and grateful acknowledgement is made to the following companies which provided reference literature used in the preparation of this book:

AC Spark Plug Division, General Motors Corporation; Auto Air Conditioning Parts Inc.; ARA Manufacturing Company; Bear Manufacturing Company; Bendix Corporation; Buick Motor Division, General Motors Corporation; Cadillac Motor Division, General Motors Corporation; Champion Spark Plug Company; Chevrolet Motor Division, General Motors Corporation; Chrysler Corporation; Delco-Moraine Inc.; Delco-Remy Division, General Motors Corporation; Delco-Rochester Products; Detroit Automotive Products; Echlin Manufacturing Company; The Electric Auto-Lite Company; FMC Corporation; Ford Motor Company; Fram Corporation; Jamco Inc.; Lee Manufacturing Company; McQuay-Norris Manufacturing Company; Moog Automotive Inc.; Nissan Motors Corporation, USA, Inc.; Perfect Circle Corporation; Purolator Products Inc.; Raybestos-Manhattan Inc.; Robinair Automotive Division; Snap-on Tools Corporation; Sun Electric Corporation; Toyota Motor Sales, USA, Inc.; TRW Products.

Grateful acknowledgment is also made to the following certified mechanics and friends who assisted in reviewing questions and offered many valuable suggestions: John Ogborn, Rio Hondo College; Clarence Bolin, Rio Hondo College; David Toft, Rio Hondo College; Alan Gettman, Rio Hondo College; Lee Haeberlein, Mountain View High School; Jeff Groves, Tweedy's Auto Electric; David Tweedy, Tweedy's Auto Electric; Bill Walsh, Board Ford; Gino Cole, McAllister Cadillac; Mark Escalante, Arrowhead-Puritas; Bill Guadagnolo, Higa's Automatic Transmission; Monty Brunk, Claude's Automotive Service; Dick Delgadillo, Dick's Front End and Brake Service; John Poochigian, Toyota Training Instructor; and Manuel Tumasian, Monterey Motors.

The author also wishes to express his thanks to his wife, Annetta, for her assistance in proofreading.

# 1

# BRAKES

STUDY OUTLINE

I. Basic Fundamentals

   A. Hydraulic System

      1. Pressure requirements

   B. Master and Wheel Cylinders
   C. Drum Brakes
   D. Disc Brakes

      1. Advantages
      2. Maintaining adjustment

   E. Power Brakes
   F. Troubleshooting


II. Hydraulic Control Devices

   A. Master Cylinder (Tandem)

      1. Operation
      2. Construction (position of parts)
      3. Nomenclature of parts
      4. Reconditioning procedures
      5. Push rod adjustment (effects)
      6. Bench bleeding
      7. Failure diagnosis

   B. Proportioning Valve

      1. Purpose
      2. Symptoms if defective

   C. Metering Valve

      1. Purpose
      2. Must be open when pressure tank bleeding
      3. Symptoms if defective

D.  Pressure Differential Switch

    1. Operation
    2. Centering
    3. Testing the dash lamp

E.  Residual Valve

    1. Purpose
    2. Drum brakes only

F.  Wheel Cylinders

    1. Nomenclature
    2. Inspection
    3. Reconditioning

G.  Brake Fluids

    1. Boiling points
    2. Water contamination

H.  Hydraulic Tubing and Hoses
I.  Anti-skid Devices


III.  System Service

A.  Bendix Type Brake

    1. Common
    2. Servo-action
    3. Nomenclature of parts (self-adjusting type)
    4. Construction (position of parts)
    5. Adjustment

B.  Drum Inspection and Reconditioning

    1. Bell-mouthing
    2. Taper
    3. Out-of-round
    4. Turning

        a. Chatter band
        b. Reason for poor finish

    5. Hard Spots

        a. Grinding

6. Scoring
7. Oversize limits
8. Drum micrometer
9. Removing drum from front hub

   a. Swaged studs

10. Wheel bearing service

C. Rotor Inspection and Use of Tools

   1. Run-out
   2. Parallelism
   3. Thickness minimum
   4. RMS finish
   5. Scoring

D. Brake Shoes

   1. Inspection

      a. Lining wear limits

   2. Arcing

      a. Purpose
      b. Oversize lining

   3. Primary and secondary shoes

E. Brake Bleeding Procedures

   1. Pressure tank

      a. Diaphragm type

   2. Manual bleeding
   3. Bleeding sequence (RR, LR, RF, LF)

F. Wheel Cylinders and Calipers

   1. Inspection
   2. Reconditioning procedures and use of tools
   3. Caliper design

      a. Fixed
      b. Floating
      c. Piston number difference

G.  Parking Brake

1. Nomenclature
2. Adjustment

IV.  Power Brakes

A.  Vacuum Suspended
B.  Atmospheric Suspended
C.  Integral, Pedal Assist, and Multiplier Types
D.  Testing/Diagnosis

1. Vacuum supply
2. Loss of fluid
3. Hard pedal
4. Rough idle with brake pedal depressed

E.  Push Rod Adjustment
F.  Purpose of Check Valve

V.  Brake Problem/Diagnosis

A.  Pulling to One Side
B.  Grabbing
C.  Chatter
D.  Pedal Pulsation (Disc and Drum)
E.  Spongy Pedal
F.  Squeals
G.  Rising Pedal (Stop Light Stays On)
H.  Low Pedal
I.  Pedal Sinks Slowly to Floor with Pressure Applied
J.  Loss of Pedal on Rough Roads (Disc)
K.  Wheel and Axle Seal Leakage
L.  Wheel Bearing Noise

VI.  Brake Service Philosophy

A.  Should Front Drums Be Turned the Same Size?
B.  How Should Lining Be Broken In?
C.  What Constitutes a Complete Brake Job?
D.  Should Pre-arced Lining Be Used?

EXERCISES

1. Mechanic A says that the part illustrated above is mounted on
   the primary brake shoe.

   Mechanic B says that the part is mounted on the secondary brake
   shoe.

   Who is right?


   a. Mechanic A
   b. Mechanic B
   c. Both A and B
   d. Neither A nor B


2. When turning a scored brake drum, the maximum oversize limit for
   most cars would be:


   a. 0.060"
   b. 0.030"
   c. 0.090"
   d. 0.110"


3. The most common type of disc brake caliper found on American cars
   since 1965 is the:


   a. Single piston sliding
   b. Two piston fixed
   c. Two piston sliding
   d. Four piston fixed

4. Some cars with front disc brakes use a metering valve.  When
   bleeding this type of brake with a pressure tank, which of the
   following apply?


   a. The metering valve plunger must be pushed to the closed position.
   b. The metering valve has no effect on bleeding brakes if a diaphragm
      type pressure tank is used.
   c. The metering valve plunger must be held in the open position.
   d. Both a and b above.

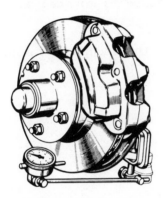

5. When making the above pictured t.i.r. check, which of the following
   readings would be considered maximum?


   a. 0.010"
   b. 0.002"
   c. 0.0005"
   d. 0.005"

6. What brake system valve is illustrated above?


   a. Pressure differential valve
   b. Metering valve
   c. Proportioning valve
   d. None of the above

7. To check rotor parallelism you use a:

    a. Straight-edge
    b. Micrometer
    c. Dial indicator
    d. Special service tool

8. A vehicle is equipped with power disc brakes. The owner says that in order to stop the car excessive pedal effort is required.

    Mechanic A says that a master cylinder or power brake malfunction could be the reason.

    Mechanic B says that air in the hydraulic system is probably the cause.

    Who is right?

    a. Mechanic A
    b. Mechanic B
    c. Both A and B
    d. Neither A nor B

9. Swollen cups in the master cylinder would indicate:

    a. Solvent contamination
    b. Denatured alcohol contamination
    c. Water contamination
    d. Both a and c above

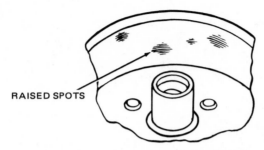

RAISED SPOTS

10. Mechanic A says that the raised surface spots shown above can be removed by turning the drum on a lathe using a carbide tool bit.

Mechanic B says that these spots can be removed by grinding. However, they may reappear when heat is applied.  The drum should really be replaced.

Who is right?

a. Mechanic A
b. Mechanic B
c. Both A and B
d. Neither A nor B

WASHER

11. The wave washer shown above is designed to:

a. Keep the secondary brake shoe from vibrating
b. Reduce parking brake lever rattle and vibration
c. Keep the primary brake shoe from vibrating
d. Reduce parking brake strut rattle and vibration

12. Drum brake fade could be caused by:

a. Improper toe-heel clearance
b. Bell-mounted drums
c. Heavily glazed lining
d. All of the above

13. If atmospheric pressure is exhausted from the power brake booster unit when the brake is being applied, the unit is of the:

    a. Atmospheric suspended type
    b. Vacuum suspended type
    c. Combination suspended type
    d. Multiplier type

14. The owner of a vehicle with front disc brakes states that the brake pedal pulsates rapidly whenever he applies the brakes. Which of the following can cause this condition?

    a. A wheel bearing not properly adjusted
    b. Uneven rotor thickness
    c. Excessive rotor t.i.r.
    d. All of the above

15. The figure 0.0005" is the dimension commonly used for maximum:

    a. Rotor lateral run-out
    b. Rotor parallelism
    c. Rotor radial run-out
    d. Caliper bore wear

16. DOT approved heavy duty brake fluid must have a minimum boiling point of:

    a. 250°F
    b. 375°F
    c. 550°F
    d. 725°F

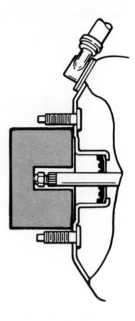

17. Mechanic A says that the above adjustment, if incorrect, can cause
    the brakes to drag.

    Mechanic B says that the above adjustment, if incorrect, can result
    in excess pedal travel.

    Who is right?


    a. Mechanic A
    b. Mechanic B
    c. Both A and B
    d. Neither A nor B


18. A honed wheel cylinder should be checked with a "No-Go" gauge,
    or inside micrometer, and should not exceed _____ over the
    original diameter.


    a. 0.002"
    b. 0.005"
    c. 0.010"
    d. 0.0005"

19. In the two-shoe, single-anchor Bendix brake, which of the following is generally true?

    a. The secondary lining is longer than the primary.
    b. The primary lining is longer than the secondary.
    c. Both linings are equal in length.
    d. None of the above are true.

20. The outer bearing race (cup) is spinning (turning) in the front hub. The customer should be sold:

    a. A new cup and bearing
    b. A new cup only
    c. A new hub only
    d. A new cup, bearing, and hub

21. When you apply the brakes hard, a car has a pull which is accompanied by a light vibration. Which of the following could cause this condition?

    a. Collapsing strut rod insulators
    b. Incorrect tire pressure
    c. Leaky wheel cylinder
    d. All of the above

22. The above illustration shows the layout of a wheel cylinder prior to assembly.

    Which item is not being installed correctly?

    a. Expander
    b. Cup
    c. Piston
    d. Boot

23. The drum brake design in wide use today is the:


    a. Duo-servo, fixed anchor
    b. Uni-servo, fixed anchor
    c. Non-servo, adjustable anchor
    d. Self-energizing, self-centering, dual anchor


24. When checking disc brake rotor lateral run-out:


    a. Remove the caliper from the steering knuckle
    b. Use a pair of calipers
    c. Use a micrometer
    d. Readjust wheel bearings when through


25. What quick method can be used to prove that the master cylinder
    compensating port is open?


    a. Check free pedal measurement.
    b. Remove filler cap, press on the brake pedal, and observe
       fluid squirt.
    c. Bleed wheel cylinder located closest to the master
       cylinder and observe fluid squirt.
    d. Both b and c above.


26. When lining brake shoes with riveted lining:


    a. Start riveting at the heel, and work toward the toe.
    b. Start riveting at the toe, and work toward the heel.
    c. Start at center and work outward in both directions.
    d. The procedure doesn't matter.


27. Problem:  You have assembled a Bendix brake with a cable self-
    adjusting mechanism.  You observe that the adjusting lever is
    below the center line of the star wheel adjuster.  A common
    cause for this is:


    a. The cable guide is not firmly seated against the secondary shoe.
    b. The cable guide is not firmly seated against the primary shoe.
    c. The cable is too short.
    d. Both a and c above.

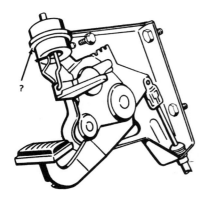

28. What best describes the function of the above part?

    a. Releases the parking brake
    b. Parking brake pivot equalizer
    c. Vacuum assist device when applying the parking brake
    d. Both a and c above.

29. On a combination brake system, which of the following could cause a pulsating brake pedal?

    a. Leaking wheel cylinder
    b. Parking brake set while the drums are hot
    c. Blocked by-pass port
    d. Glazed linings

30. When holding your foot on the brake, the pedal drops slightly when the engine is started.

    Mechanic A says that this is a sign of a faulty power brake booster.

    Mechanic B says that this is normal on a car with a power assisted dual master cylinder.

    Who is right?

    a. A only
    b. B only
    c. Either A or B
    d. Neither A nor B

31. The type of power brake system which has a self-contained
    hydraulic cylinder "slaved" to the master cylinder is:

    a. An integral type
    b. A pressure multiplier type
    c. A pedal assist type
    d. An oil-over-air type

32. The rubber strap wrapped around the brake drum during turning on
    the lathe is to:

    a. Cool the drum
    b. Shield operator from flying chips
    c. Prevent drum expansion
    d. Reduce chatter

33. The master cylinder maintains residual pressure on a drum brake
    system in order to:

    a. Keep the wheel cylinder cups sealed against the cylinder bores
    b. Prevent air from entering the system
    c. Both A and B
    d. Neither A nor B

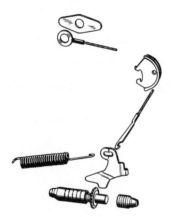

34. According to the illustration above, these parts would be for the:

    a. Front brakes
    b. Rear brakes
    c. Right side brakes
    d. Left side brakes

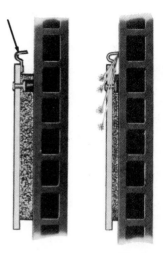

**NEW PAD          WORN PAD**

35. The arrow in the picture above is pointing to:


    a. An anti-rattle clip
    b. A stabilizer
    c. An anchor plate
    d. A wear indicator


36. Disc brakes normally use no residual pressure check valve because:


    a. Disc brakes use a metering valve
    b. Residual pressure would cause dragging of brakes
    c. Residual pressure would delay front brake application
    d. Disc brakes use a proportioning valve


37. Prior to replacing disc brake pads, remove some of the brake fluid
    from the master cylinder reservoir that feeds the disc brakes.
    This will:


    a. Make bleeding easier
    b. Prevent fluid overflow when the pistons are pushed back into
       the calipers
    c. Allow pressure to the front and rear axles to equalize
    d. Prevent the brake warning light from coming on

38. The owner of an American passenger car complains of a pull to
    the right when he steps on the brakes.

    Mechanic A says the trouble could be caused by the master cylinder
    (dual type).

    Mechanic B says the trouble could be a faulty metering or propor-
    tioning valve.

    Who is right?


    a. Mechanic A
    b. Mechanic B
    c. Either A or B
    d. Neither A nor B


39. The disc brake reservoir portion of a dual master cylinder is low
    on fluid.

    Mechanic A says the brake pads may be worn.

    Mechanic B says the power brake booster may be faulty.

    Who is right?


    a. A only
    b. B only
    c. Both A and B
    d. Neither A nor B


40. A firm, steady pressure on the brake pedal results in the pedal
    slowly sinking to the floor.  No external fluid leaks can be
    detected.  What is the most likely cause?


    a. Leaking secondary cup
    b. Defective residual check valve
    c. Plugged inlet port
    d. Leaking primary cup

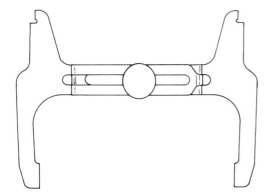

41. Mechanic A says that the above tool sets correct lining-to-drum
    clearance on cars using the Bendix type fixed anchor self-adjusting
    brake.

    Mechanic B says that the above tool sets correct toe and heel
    clearance.

Who is right?


    a. Mechanic A
    b. Mechanic B
    c. Both A and B
    d. Neither A nor B


42. When a brake drum has been turned 0.050" over OEM size, and the
    brake shoes are standard, which of the following will apply?


    a. The shoes will contact the drum at the ends only.
    b. The shoes will fit the drum properly.
    c. The shoes will contact the drum at the center only.
    d. The shoes should be arc ground only on the ends.

43. What operation is the mechanic performing in the above picture?

    a. Installing square-cut seal
    b. Installing caliper piston
    c. Installing dust boot
    d. None of the above

44. When bleeding the brakes, you would normally start with the wheel cylinder or caliper:

    a. Closest to the master cylinder
    b. Farthest from the master cylinder
    c. On the same side as the master cylinder
    d. On the right front side

45. When using a pressure tank for bleeding drum type brakes, which of the following pressures would you use?

    a. 2 to 8 psi
    b. 15 to 30 psi
    c. 40 to 65 psi
    d. 60 to 80 psi

46. On drum type brakes, which of the following could cause a rising pedal on successive brake applications?

    a. Insufficient pedal free travel
    b. Master cylinder piston not returning to its stop
    c. Both a and b
    d. Neither a nor b

47. To comply with OSHA standards, the arcing of linings should be done only if:

    a. The mechanic wears safety glasses
    b. The mechanic wears a respirator
    c. Dust is vacuumed away as it is created
    d. All of the above take place

48. Most combination brake systems use a proportioning valve.  Its purpose is to:

    a. Act as a safety valve with the dual type master cylinder
    b. Reduce pressure at the front brakes
    c. Reduce pressure at the rear brakes
    d. Act as a cut-off valve in the event of front or rear system failure

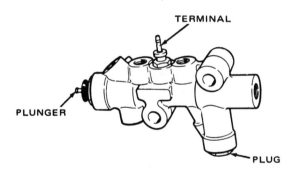

49. Mechanic A says that the above valve assembly actuates the brake warning lamp.

    Mechanic B says that the above valve assembly delays pressure build-up to the front axle disc brakes.

    Who is right?

    a. Mechanic A
    b. Mechanic B
    c. Both A and B
    d. Neither A nor B

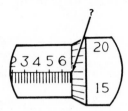

50. What is the above micrometer reading?

    a. 0.647
    b. 0.683
    c. 0.698
    d. None of the above


51. A plugged master cylinder filler cap vent can cause:

    a. Brake fluid to be forced out through the secondary cup in the
       master cylinder
    b. A spongy brake pedal
    c. The brakes to drag
    d. None of the above


52. On a front disc brake vehicle, violent cornering or rough roads may
    cause:

    a. A drop in fluid pressure
    b. Excessive pedal travel
    c. Both a and b
    c. Neither a nor b


53. On a slick road condition, what prevents the front disc brakes
    from locking up at light pedal pressures before the drum brakes
    develop sufficient stopping force?

    a. Proportioning valve
    b. By-pass valve
    c. Residual valve
    d. Metering valve

54. Mechanic A says that master cylinders used on a disc/drum combina-
    tion system have a smaller reservoir for the front disc brakes than
    they do for the rear drum brakes.

    Mechanic B says that the disc brake rotors in a combination system
    have a lower pressure requirement than the rear drums.

    Who is right?

    a. Mechanic A
    b. Mechanic B
    c. Both A and B
    d. Neither A nor B

55. You are replacing the brake lining on a two-shoe, single-anchor
    Bendix type brake. Brake drum diameter measures 10.045". When
    you are grinding the shoe surface, which of the following diameters
    would you use?

    a. 10.000"
    b. 10.015"
    c. 10.045"
    d. 10.060"

56. When replacing a hydraulic brake line, which of the following is
    correct procedure?

    a. Use seamless copper tubing with single flared ends.
    b. Cut out bad section, install steel tubing using a union.
    c. Use single length double flared steel or copper tubing.
    d. None of the above.

57. Many late model brake systems use the above rubber diaphragm.
    What is its function?

    a. To eliminate the need for a residual check valve
    b. To maintain static pressure
    c. To prevent water and dirt contamination
    d. To allow for "brake pedal pump-up" if the pedal is low

58. The above pictured drum was turned at too fast a feed.  This
    condition will cause:

    a. Low-speed squeal
    b. A snapping noise as brakes are applied
    c. Vibration
    d. Fade

59. Which of the following would be a desired RMS surface finish for
    a disc brake rotor?

    a. 80 to 100
    b. 15 to 80
    c. 0 to 15
    d. 100 to 280

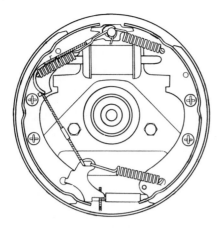

60. Refer to the above brake assembly illustration.  In which direction must the drum turn in order to operate the self-adjusting mechanism?

    a. Clockwise
    b. Counter-clockwise
    c. Either direction
    d. Not enough information given to correctly answer question

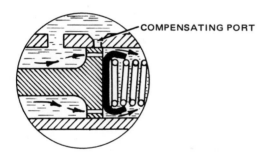

61. Mechanic A says that the above illustration (single piston master cylinder) shows fluid flow during brake application.

    Mechanic B says that fluid flow during fast release is shown.

    Who is right?

    A. Mechanic A
    b. Mechanic B
    c. Both A and B
    d. Neither A nor B

62. Identify the above item:


    a. Disc brake stabilizer plate
    b. Caliper retaining clip
    c. Brake hose lock
    d. Brake cable equalizer clip

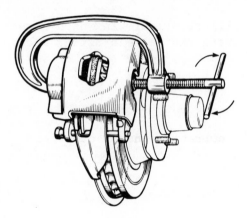

63. The above illustration shows the:


    a. Caliper mounting pin being pressed out
    b. Caliper piston being pushed into its bore
    c. Outboard shoe being attached to the caliper
    d. Outer shoe ears being crimped

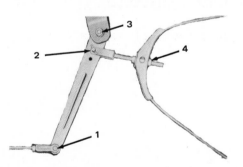

64. Refer to the arrows in the above drawing and indicate where the
    parking brake adjustment is usually made:


    a. #1
    b. #2
    c. #3
    d. #4

65. The above illustration shows the layout of a single piston master cylinder prior to assembly.

    Which item is not in correct position?

    a. Check valve
    b. Primary cup
    c. Piston
    d. Secondary cup

66. The above illustration shows:

    a. Two types of proportioning valves
    b. Two types of metering valves
    c. Neither a metering valve nor a proportioning valve
    d. A metering valve and a proportioning valve

67. The above tool can be used to simplify which of the following operations?

    a. Bleeding
    b. Caliper sleeve installation
    c. Caliper guide pin alignment
    d. Setting master cylinder push rod clearance

←— PIECE OF WOOD

68. The above illustration shows the:

    a. Caliper-to-piston-bore clearance being checked
    b. Piston being removed from caliper
    c. Dust boot and piston being installed
    d. Square-cut seal being removed

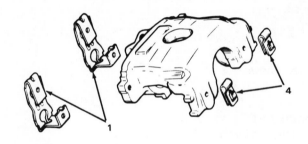

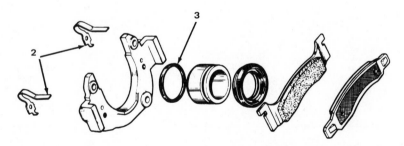

69. Refer to the above disc brake exploded view illustration. Which arrow
    is pointing to the part(s) responsible for the self-adjusting action?

    a. #1
    b. #2
    c. #3
    d. #4

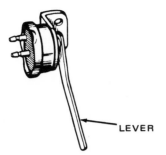

LEVER

70. Mechanic A says that the above switch can be tested by using a jumper wire to by-pass it.

    Mechanic B says that the above switch can be tested by grounding either terminal.

    Who is right?


    a. Mechanic A
    b. Mechanic B
    c. Both A and B
    d. Neither A nor B

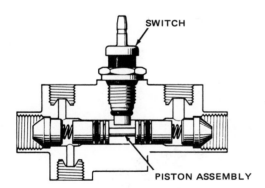

SWITCH

PISTON ASSEMBLY

71. Mechanic A says that the above switch completes a ground circuit.

    Mechanic B says that the piston shown above will be displaced during bleeding, but will recenter itself after pressure is decreased below a certain point by releasing the brake pedal.

    Who is right?


    a. Mechanic A
    b. Mechanic B
    c. Both A and B
    d. Neither A nor B

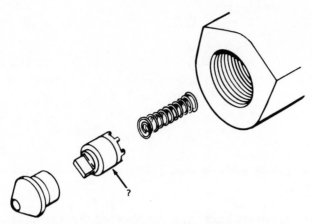

72. The arrow in the above illustration is pointing to:


    a. A disc brake residual check valve
    b. A disc brake by-pass valve
    c. A drum brake residual check valve
    d. None of the above

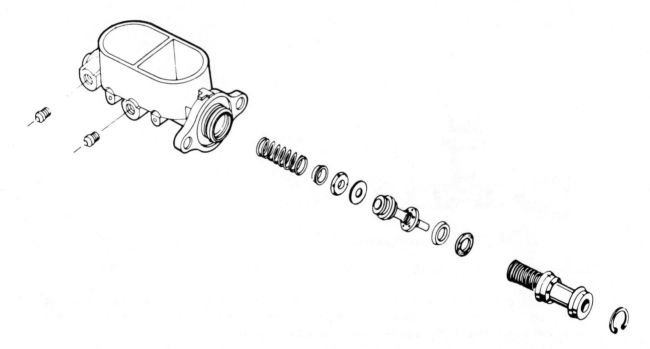

73. Refer to the above master cylinder illustration.  Which part is not
    in correct position?


    a. Primary piston
    b. Secondary piston
    c. Primary seal
    d. Tube seat inserts

74. The residual check valve:

    I. Holds about 8 to 16 psi in the drum brake cylinders
   II. Holds about 8 to 16 psi in the disc brake calipers

    a. I only
    b. II only
    c. Both I and II
    d. Neither I nor II

75. According to the National Traffic and Motor Vehicle Safety Act,
all American passenger cars starting with the 1970 models must have:

    I. A tandem master cylinder
   II. A warning device that indicates pressure differences between
      the two systems.

    a. I only
    b. II only
    c. Both I and II
    d. Neither I nor II

76. The advantages of a sliding caliper on disc brakes are:

    a. None, just manufacturer's choice
    b. That it compensates for slight disc warp and has actuating
      cylinders on one side of caliper only
    c. That it is heavier and will dissipate heat faster
    d. That it permits the use of a much heavier disc

77. On the duo-servo brake with a lever type self-adjuster, the above
    part is mounted on the:


    I. Secondary brake shoe
    II. Primary brake shoe


    a. I only
    b. II only
    c. Either I or II
    d. Neither I nor II


78. Which  of the following front wheel bearing settings would you
    consider to be correct for a vehicle equipped with disc brakes?


    a. 12 inch lbs. - back off one flat
    b. 90 foot lbs. - back off one flat
    c. 0.000" - 0.003" end play
    d. 0.010" - 0.020" end play

# 2

# FRONT ENDS

STUDY OUTLINE

I.  Front End Types and Construction

    A.  Solid Axle Front End

        1.  King pin and steering knuckle
        2.  Linkage component identification

    B.  Independent Front Suspension

        1.  Lower coil spring mount
        2.  Upper coil spring mount
        3.  Torsion bar
        4.  Nomenclature of parts

    C.  MacPherson Strut Suspension
    D.  Twin I-Beam Design


II.  Types of Springs

    A.  Leaf

        1.  Rebound clip
        2.  Center bolt
        3.  Shackle
        4.  Tapered single leaf

    B.  Coil

        1.  Should be replaced in pairs
        2.  Curb height specifications

    C.  Torsion Bar

        1.  Adjustable

    D.  Controlling Spring Oscillation

        1.  Function of shock absorber

III.  Alignment Factors

    A.  Caster
    B.  Camber
    C.  Toe-in
    D.  Steering Axis Inclination (S.A.I.)
    E.  Toe-out on Turns (Turning Radius)
    F.  Included Angle
    G.  Steering Wheel Centering
    H.  Point of Intersection


IV.  Alignment Angle Effects

    A.  Caster

        1. Positive or negative
        2. A directional control angle
        3. Wander and weave
        4. Stability
        5. Turning effort
        6. Returnability
        7. Road crown pull

    B.  Camber

        1. Positive or negative
        2. Is a tire wearing angle
        3. Pulling (wander)
        4. Provides for easy steering
        5. Brings road contact point of tire more nearly under point of
           load

    C.  Toe-in

        1. Purpose
        2. Tire wear (feather edging)
        3. Stability

    D.  Steering Axis Inclination

        1. Provides a pivot point to produce easier steering
        2. Reduces need for excessive camber
        3. Effect on wheel bearings
        4. Non-adjustable

E.  Toe-out on Turns

1. Built-in design angle (steering arms)
2. Purpose
3. Greater angle on inside wheel
4. Oversteering and understeering
5. Tire wear (scuffing)

V.  Rear Suspension Systems

A.  Function of Components

1. "U" bolts
2. Control arms
3. Stabilizer bar
4. Controlling "wrap-up"

B.  Rear Wheel Alignment

1. Tracking
2. Tram gauges
3. Setting camber

VI.  Front Suspension Service

A.  Inspection

1. Ball joints

a. Load carrying
b. Follower
c. Compression
d. Tension
e. Jacking points
f. Wear indicator type joint
g. Axial and radial movement

2. Idler Arms

a. Types
b. Installation (wheels straight ahead)

3. Control arm bushings
4. Pivot shaft
5. Tie rod ends
6. Relay rod (center link)
7. Pitman arm

8. Sway bar and linkage
9. Strut rod bushings
10. Wheel bearings/adjustments

B. Alignment

1. Sequence procedure for alignment
2. Method of adjustment for caster and camber

   a. Shims (understand adjustment location)
   b. Eccentrics (cams on control arm)
   c. Serrated/slotted cross shaft
   d. Strut rods
   e. Cold bending (solid axles)

3. Toe-in

   a. Scribing the tire
   b. Adjusting sleeve tool
   c. Left hand and right hand threads
   d. Centering steering wheel

4. Toe-out on turns

   a. Left (outside wheel) turn in 20°
   b. Right (inside wheel) should read?

5. Equipment identification and use

   a. Magnetic gauge
   b. Radius plate
   c. Brake pedal jack
   d. Toe gauge
   e. Steering wheel holder
   f. Wheel run-out gauge
   g. Scuff gauge

VII. Wheels and Tires

A. Run-out

1. Radial
2. Lateral
3. Specifications

B. Effects of Wheels and Tires Not Within Specifications
C. Tire Tread Wear Patterns and Causes

D. Wheel Balance

1. Static
2. Dynamic
3. Tramp
4. Shimmy

E. Tire Rotation Patterns

1. Bias belted
2. Radial

VIII. Problem/Diagnosis

A. Idler Arm Wear
B. A-arm Bushing Wear
C. Ball Joint Wear
D. Pulling
E. Wheel Shimmy
F. Wheel Tramp
G. Handling Characteristics Poor

1. Interpreting wheel alignment readings and charts

H. Wheel Run-out

IX. Steering Gears

A. Manual

1. Types
2. Adjustments

a. Lash
b. Preload

3. Diagnosis

a. Hard steering
b. Looseness
c. Roughness
d. Binding through the center of travel

B. Power

1. Types

2. Diagnosis

    a. Hard steering (reduced assist)
    b. Loss of fluid (leakage points)
    c. Checking procedures
    d. Noises
    e. Checking pump pressures
    f. Pull
    g. Poor returnability out of a turn

3. Adjustments

    a. Worm bearing preload (torsion bar feel)
    b. Sector (ball nut) mesh
    c. Centering shims (spool valve)
    d. Pump belt tension

---

EXERCISES

1. Which of the following is not considered a tire wearing angle?

    a. Caster
    b. Camber
    c. Toe-in
    d. Turning radius

2. A car turns a corner.  Which of the following statements is true?

    a. The inside wheel turns at a greater angle.
    b. The outside wheel turns at a greater angle.
    c. Both wheels turn at equal angles.
    d. None of the above

3. What are the effects of toe not being set correctly?

    a. A little too much toe-in can result in wear on the outside of
       the right front tire.
    b. A little too much toe-out can result in wear on the inside of
       the left front tire.
    c. Toe-in wear usually results in a feather edge on the tire tread.
    d. All of the above

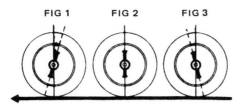

FIG 1    FIG 2    FIG 3

FRONT OF CAR

4. Refer to the above illustration.  Which of the following statements
   is correct?


   a. Figure 1 shows negative caster.
   b. Figure 2 shows zero caster.
   c. Figure 3 shows positive caster.
   d. All of the above


5. A customer complains of front wheel "shimmy."  This could be
   caused by:


   a. Dynamic imbalance
   b. Static imbalance
   c. Either a or b
   d. Neither a nor b


6. Which of the following would be a cause of wheel "tramp"?


   a. Dynamic imbalance
   b. Static imbalance
   c. Either a or b
   d. Neither a nor b


7. The purpose of S.A.I. is:

   a. To help offset road crown pull
   b. To help reduce the need for excessive camber
   c. To keep the camber and caster angles constant when the vehicle
      is in motion
   d. All of the above

8. When correcting for static imbalance, the total amount of required weight is generally divided equally between the inside and outside of the rim.  This is done to:

   a. Help prevent vertical shake
   b. Help prevent wheel "tramp"
   c. Help prevent the creation of dynamic imbalance
   d. All of the above

9. A customer wants the wheels balanced on his four-wheel drive vehicle.

   Mechanic A says that the recommended procedure is to use an off-car balancer.

   Mechanic B says that the recommended procedure is to use an electronic on-car balancer.

   Who is right?

   a. Mechanic A
   b. Mechanic B
   c. Either A or B
   d. Neither A nor B

10. You are installing an idler arm with compressed rubber (molded) bushings.  Where should the wheels be positioned during installation?

    a. To the left
    b. To the right
    c. Straight ahead
    d. To the right and touching the ground

11. You pass your hand across a tire from the inside to the outside. You feel a sharp and ragged feather edge.  This condition is caused by:

    a. Excessive toe-in
    b. Excessive toe-out
    c. Either a or b
    d. Neither a nor b

12. Mechanic A says that too much negative caster can cause wander, weave, and instability at high speeds.

    Mechanic B says that too much positive caster can cause hard steering, excessive road shock, and shimmy.

    Who is right?

    a. Mechanic A
    b. Mechanic B
    c. Both A and B
    d. Neither A nor B

13. You have just aligned the front end of a car. The owner weighs 250 lbs. When he sits down behind the steering wheel:

    a. Camber on the left wheel will increase toward positive.
    b. Camber on the right wheel will increase toward positive.
    c. Camber on both wheels becomes more positive.
    d. Camber on both wheels becomes more negative.

14. A very heavy load is placed in the trunk of a car.

    Mechanic A says that front wheel caster will increase toward positive.

    Mechanic B says that camber of both front wheels will decrease toward negative.

    Who is right?

    a. Mechanic A
    b. Mechanic B
    c. Both A and B
    d. Neither A nor B

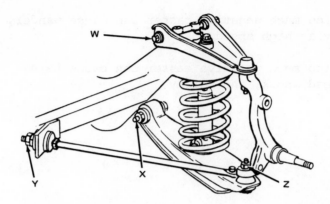

15. Refer to the above illustration.  Where is the caster adjustment
    usually made on this type of suspension system?


    a. Point W
    b. Point X
    c. Point Y
    d. Point Z


16. Which of the following is true of the conventional shock absorber?


    a. It dampens out spring oscillations.
    b. A worn or leaky shock will not cause a car to lean.
    c. Purge air from new shocks before installing.
    d. All of the above


17. Standing height (curb height) should be equal on both sides of a
    car within:


    a. 1/16"
    b. 1/2"
    c. 1"
    d. 2"

FIG 1            FIG 2

FRONT VIEW

18. Refer to the above illustration.  Which of the following statements
    are true?

    a. Figure 1 shows negative camber.
    b. Figure 2 shows positive camber.
    c. Figure 1 and 2 show negative camber.
    d. None of the above

19. Mechanic A says that a vehicle will have a tendency to pull to
    the side having the most positive camber.

    Mechanic B says that it will pull to the side having the least
    positive caster.

    Who is right?

    a. Mechanic A
    b. Mechanic B
    c. Both A and B
    d. Neither A nor B

20. Inspection reveals a weak front coil spring.  What would be recom-
    mended service procedure?

    Mechanic A says to replace both front springs.

    Mechanic B says to replace only the weak spring.

    Who is right?

    a. Mechanic A
    b. Mechanic B
    c. Either A or B
    d. Neither A nor B

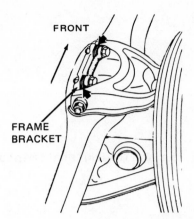

FRONT

FRAME
BRACKET

21. In the above illustration, what would the mechanic do to change camber to a more positive angle without changing caster?

    a. Remove an equal thickness of shims from the front and the rear shim pack.
    b. Add an equal thickness of shims to the front and the rear shim pack.
    c. Add shims to the rear shim pack only.
    d. Remove shims from the front shim pack, and add an equal thickness to the rear shim pack.

22. A car is equipped with power steering. The owner complains of a pull to the right side. What could be the cause?

    a. Improper wheel alignment
    b. Internal leakage in the steering gear control valve
    c. Both a and b
    d. Neither a nor b

23. Mechanic A says that incorrect negative camber will produce outside tire tread wear.

Mechanic B says that excessive unequal camber between wheels will cause a pull to one side.

Who is right?

    a. Mechanic A
    b. Mechanic B
    c. Both A and B
    d. Neither A nor B

24. Which one of the following items is not a means of adjusting
    camber on a vehicle?

    a. A cam-bolt assembly
    b. A strut rod
    c. A sliding control arm shaft
    d. Shims

25. Mechanic A says that sagged steering linkage can cause hidden
    toe change when the vehicle is in motion.

    Mechanic B says that the toe-in setting is the most critical tire
    wearing angle.

    Who is right?

    a. Mechanic A
    b. Mechanic B
    c. Both A and B
    d. Neither A nor B

26. The caster on the left wheel has been set at 1-3/4° negative.  The
    right wheel caster has been set at 7/8° negative.  What would more
    than likely result?

    a. The car would pull to the right.
    b. The car would pull to the left.
    c. The car would travel straight ahead.
    d. The left tire would show second rib wear.

27. When taking a caster reading with the above type gauge, the wheel is:


    a. Turned through a 40° arc
    b. Locked in a straight-ahead position
    c. Turned through a 20° arc
    d. Rolled 180°

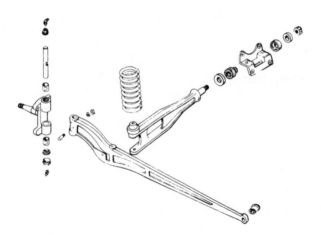

28. Camber is adjusted on the above front suspension assembly by:


    a. Turning the nut on the end of the radius arm
    b. Cold bending the axle
    c. Heating the axle with a torch and bending
    d. Turning the axle pivot bushing

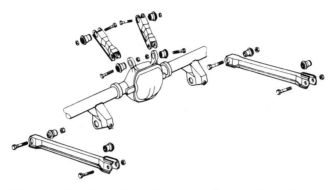

29. Rear axle housing "wrap-up" on the above type of suspension system is controlled by:


    a. The coil springs
    b. The rebound clips
    c. The control arms
    d. The center bolts

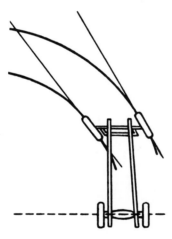

30. The above drawing illustrates a vehicle making a left turn.  The left wheel is turning at a 20° angle.  As a general rule the right wheel would then be turning at:


    a. 17°
    b. 20°
    c. 23°
    d. 30°

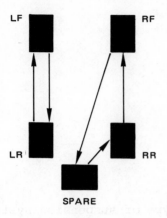

31. The above tire rotation pattern is generally used for:


    a. Bias tires
    b. Bias-belted tires
    c. Radial tires
    d. Nylon tires


32. When performing a wheel alignment, which adjustment is generally
    made first?


    a. Toe-in
    b. Camber
    c. Caster
    d. Turning radius


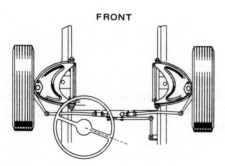

33. The steering wheel spoke in the above picture is low on the right
    side.  If the toe-in is correct, what is required to center the wheel?


    a. Shorten the right tie rod.
    b. Lengthen the left tie rod.
    c. Lengthen the left tie rod and shorten the right tie rod.
    d. Shorten the left tie rod and lengthen the right tie rod.

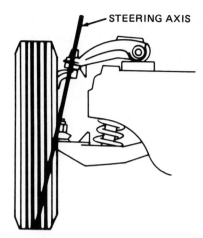

34. Refer to the above picture. Ball joint inclination is equal
    to:

    a. The included angle minus the camber angle
    b. The included angle plus the camber angle
    c. The camber angle
    d. The true vertical

35. Mechanic A says that the measurement of turning radius checks the
    accuracy of the caster and toe adjustment.

    Mechanic B says that this measurement checks for bent, damaged,
    or worn steering components.

    Who is right?

    a. Mechanic A
    b. Mechanic B
    c. Both A and B
    d. Neither A nor B

36. Which one of the following would you consider to be a typical
    front-end camber specification?

    a. - 4½°
    b. + 6°
    c. 1/8"
    d. + ¼°

37. When rear axle misalignment is suspected, you can check rear wheel camber and toe-in. Which of the following would indicate factory original settings on the rear of most vehicles?

    a. Camber +¼; toe-in 3/16 inch
    b. Camber 0; toe-in 1/8 inch
    c. Camber 0; toe-in 0 inch
    d. Camber +¼; toe-in 0 inch

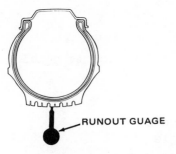

RUNOUT GUAGE

38. When performing the above radial runout check, what is generally considered the maximum allowed?

    a. 1/6"
    b. .040"
    c. .125"
    d. 1/4"

39. The above tool is used for:

    a. Setting torsion bar height
    b. Removing and installing control arm bushings
    c. Removing and installing press fit type ball joints
    d. Compressing coil springs

40. On a wear indicator type ball joint (see above), replace the joint when:

    a. The grease fitting boss projects 0.050" from the base plate.
    b. The boss becomes flush with the base plate.
    c. The boss is recessed into the base plate.
    d. Both b and c are correct.

41. Mechanic A says that ball joints are threaded into the control arms.

    Mechanic B says that ball joints are pressed into the control arms.

    Who is right?

    a. Mechanic A
    b. Mechanic B
    c. Both A and B
    d. Neither A nor B

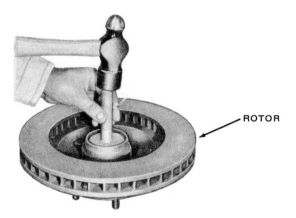

ROTOR

42. The above picture shows a mechanic:

    a. Installing the front wheel grease seal
    b. Removing the inner wheel bearing cup
    c. Installing the inner wheel bearing cup
    d. Installing the outer wheel bearing cup

43. The above picture shows a steering wheel being removed from a collapsible column.

Mechanic A says that this type of puller will damage the column.

Mechanic B says that a knock-off type of puller should be used.

Who is right?


a. Mechanic A
b. Mechanic B
c. Both A and B
d. Neither A nor B


44. On a F70-14 tire, what does the "70" indicate?


a. The height is 70% of the width
b. The width is 70% of the height
c. The tire traction rating
d. The load range rating


45. If the upper ball joints are positioned ahead of the lower ball joints, the tires have:


a. Negative camber
b. Positive camber
c. Negative caster
d. Positive caster

46. When the rear of the front tires are closer together than at the
    front, the tires have:


    a. Negative camber
    b. Positive camber
    c. Toe-in
    d. Toe-out

47. What is the name of the above part?


    a. Steering linkage stabilizer
    b. Steering damper
    c. Power cylinder
    d. Power steering control valve

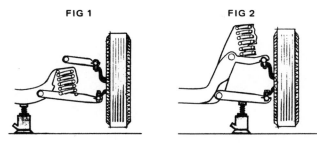

48. To check for ball joint wear, the vehicle must be lifted a certain
    way. Which statement is true regarding the above illustrations?


    a. Fig. 1 and 2 show correct procedure.
    b. Fig. 1 and 2 show incorrect procedure.
    c. Fig. 1 is correct.
    d. Fig. 2 is correct.

FIG 1          FIG 2

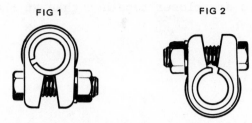

49. Which tie rod clamp position above is correct?


   a. Fig. 1 and 2 are correct.
   b. Fig. 1 and 2 are incorrect.
   c. Fig. 1 is correct.
   d. Fig. 2 is correct.

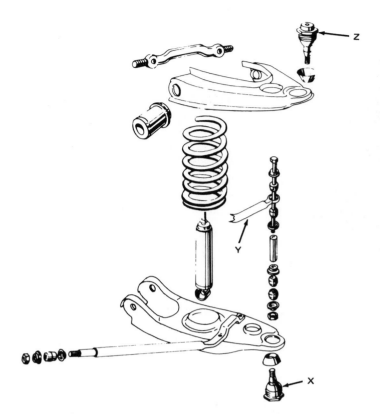

50. Mechanic A says that the follower ball joint in the above type of suspension is located at point X.

    Mechanic B says that it is located at point Z.

    Who is right?


    a. Mechanic A
    b. Mechanic B
    c. Either A or B
    d. Neither A nor B


51. Refer to the drawing for question 50.  What is the name of the part to which arrow Y points?


    a. Relay rod
    b. Torsion bar
    c. Strut rod
    d. Stabilizer bar

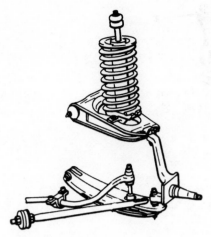

52. You are checking the load carrying ball joint for wear on the
    above suspension system.

    Mechanic A says to place a jack under the frame.

    Mechanic B says to place a wedge between the frame and upper
    control arm.

    Who is right?

    a. Mechanic A
    b. Mechanic B
    c. Both A and B
    d. Neither A nor B


53. The axial wear measurement of a ball joint is the movement:


    a. Up and down
    b. Sideways
    c. In a horizontal direction
    d. In a radial direction


54. The center bolt:


    a. Holds the leaf spring to the axle housing
    b. Holds the leaf spring together
    c. Holds the leaf spring together and locates the spring
    d. Positions the shackle assembly in the spring eye bushing

55. Unsprung weight refers to:

    a. The GVW rating
    b. Weight not supported by the springs
    c. Weight not attached to the springs
    d. Weight supported by the springs

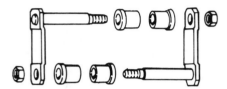

56. What is the purpose of the above parts assembly?

    a. To dampen vibration and noise
    b. To compensate for spring length changes
    c. To minimize body roll
    d. To limit jounce and rebound

57. The purpose of a torsion bar in a power steering gearbox is to:

    a. Provide "feel" for the driver
    b. Help absorb road shock
    c. Give maximum assist when required
    d. Maintain preload on the worm bearing

58. A vehicle is equipped with an integral power steering system. The
    owner complains of hard steering. A pressure gauge hooked into the
    system reads 250 psi when the hand valve is closed.

    Mechanic A says that the problem is in the pump.

    Mechanic B says that the problem is in the steering gearbox.

    Who is right?

    a. Mechanic A
    b. Mechanic B
    c. Either A or B
    d. Neither A nor B

59. A customer complains of poor steering wheel return when going
    around a corner.

    Mechanic A says that under-inflated tires could be the cause.

    Mechanic B says that incorrect alignment angles could be the cause.

    Who is right?


    a. Mechanic A
    b. Mechanic B
    c. Both A and B
    d. Neither A nor B


60. A power steering equipped car makes a "squealing" noise (particularly
    when parking).

    Mechanic A says that a loose drive belt could be the cause.

    Mechanic B says that low oil level in the pump could be the cause.

    Who is right?


    a. Mechanic A
    b. Mechanic B
    c. Both A and B
    d. Neither A nor B


61. A "binding" is felt when the steering wheel is turned through the
    center position.  What adjustment is wrong?


    a. Cross shaft end play
    b. Worm shaft end play
    c. Hi-point
    d. Worm bearing preload


62. In the linkage type power steering system, which statement below is true?


    a. The end of the pitman arm actuates a spool valve.
    b. The control valve is built into the steering gearbox.
    c. The assist cylinder is built into the steering gearbox.
    d. All of the above

63. Bleeding a power steering system is accomplished by:

    a. Opening a bleeder valve
    b. Removing the pressure line
    c. Removing the return line
    d. Turning the steering wheel

64. In a recirculating ball type steering gearbox, the teeth on the sector (pitman) shaft are meshed with:

    a. The ball nut teeth
    b. The worm gear
    c. The steering shaft gear
    d. None of the above

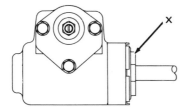

65. What steering gearbox adjustment is made at point X?

    a. Worm preload
    b. Spool valve centering
    c. Lash
    d. None of the above

66. One procedure that is almost always recommended when adjusting a steering gearbox is:

    a. Raise front wheels off the shop floor.
    b. Inflate front tires to correct pressure.
    c. Disconnect the pitman arm from the sector shaft.
    d. Make adjustments 45° from the right or left stop.

ROLLER

67. The tool pictured above is a:

    a. Tracking gauge
    b. Ball joint wear gauge
    c. Spindle run-out gauge
    d. Torsion bar adjustment gauge

68. Mechanic A says that on some vehicles .070" is acceptable axial movement for a load-carrying ball joint.

Mechanic B says that on some vehicles .100" is an acceptable axial movement specification.

Who is right?

    a. Mechanic A
    b. Mechanic B
    c. Both A and B
    d. Neither A nor B

69. Caster spread on the front wheels of most cars should not exceed:

    a. 1/2°
    b. 1/4°
    c. 1°
    d. 3/4°

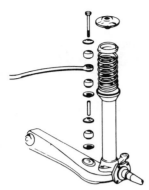

70. The above type of suspension is known as the:

    a. Panhard design
    b. Torsion bar design
    c. MacPherson strut design
    d. Long-and-short arm design

71. You are pressure testing a unitized (integral) power steering
    system.  The engine is idling and the gauge hand valve is open.
    The steering wheel is turned from extreme left to extreme right.
    The pressure readings obtained at each extreme are different.

    Mechanic A says that a seal could be leaking within the gearbox unit.

    Mechanic B says that the pump flow control valve could be sticking
    open.

    Who is right?

    a. Mechanic A
    b. Mechanic B
    c. Either A or B
    d. Neither A nor B

72. You are aligning a vehicle that has front and rear radial tires.
    It was originally equipped with conventional tires.  What front
    wheel settings are generally recommended in this situation?

    a. Minimum toe-in setting as specified by vehicle manufacturer
    b. Maximum positive caster as specified
    c. Minimum camber setting as specified
    d. All of the above

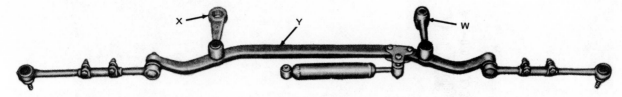

73. Refer to the above illustrated steering linkage.  Which statement
    is correct?

    a. The pitman arm is located at point W.
    b. The idler arm is located at point X.
    c. The center link is located at point Y.
    d. All of the above

74. If the steering wheel spoke is in correct position, how should
    toe-in be adjusted?

    a. At the right tie rod sleeve
    b. At the left tie rod sleeve
    c. Lengthen or shorten both tie rods equally.
    d. Either a or b

75. Mechanic A says that cupped tires can be caused by faulty shock
    absorbers.

    Mechanic B says that wheels or tires out of balance can be a
    cause of tire cupping.

    Who is right?

    a. Mechanic A
    b. Mechanic B
    c. Both A and B
    d. Neither A nor B

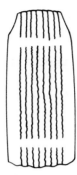

76. What does the above tire wear pattern indicate?

    a. Over-inflation wear
    b. Under-inflation wear
    c. Cornering wear
    d. The tread depth is approximately 1/16" and the tire needs to be replaced.

77. Mechanic A says that the purpose of camber is to provide easy steering by having the vehicle weight supported by the inner wheel bearing.

    Mechanic B says that the purpose of camber is to bring the road contact of the tire more nearly under the point of load.

    Who is right?

    a. Mechanic A
    b. Mechanic B
    c. Both A and B
    d. Neither A nor B

78. Which of the following statements is true regarding the front wheel bearing assembly?

    a. If a cone and roller assembly is defective, replace the cup also.
    b. Generally, tapered roller wheel bearings require no preloading.
    c. The grease seal should be replaced when packing or replacing wheel bearings.
    d. All of the above

79. Why is caster designed into the front wheels of an automobile?

  a. To maintain vehicle directional control by causing the front
     wheels to maintain a straight-ahead position
  b. To cause the wheels to return to a straight-ahead position out
     of a turn
  c. To offset road crown
  d. All of the above

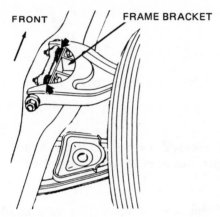

80. With reference to the above illustration, which statement is true?

  a. Removing an equal number of shims from the front and the rear
     will make camber more positive.
  b. Removing shims from the front shim pack only will make caster
     more positive.
  c. Both a and b
  d. Neither a nor b

81. You need to correct a road crown pull condition.  What would you do?

  a. Set both front wheels with equal positive caster.
  b. Place more camber, toward negative, on the left wheel.
  c. Place more caster, toward negative, on the right wheel.
  d. Place more caster, toward positive, on the right wheel.

82. A vehicle is equipped with power steering. The owner complains of a "buzzing" noise when the engine is running at a fast idle speed. As soon as the wheels are turned the noise disappears. What is the most possible cause?

    a. Loose belt
    b. Restricted hose
    c. Sticking flow control valve
    d. Scored pump bearing shaft

# 3

# ENGINE REPAIR

STUDY OUTLINE

I.  Engine Systems

    A.  Four Stroke Cycle

        1. Intake
        2. Compression
        3. Power
        4. Exhaust

    B.  Engine Design

        1. Cylinders in-line
        2. V-Type block advantages
        3. Overhead camshaft

            a. Advantages
            b. How driven?

        4. Various valve locations

            a. "I" head most common
            b. Others

        5. Valve timing

            a. Opening and closing points with reference to crankpin position
            b. What is valve overlap?

    C.  Cylinder Assembly

        1. Crankshafts

            a. 90° crankpin spacing on a V-8
            b. Vibration damper purpose
            c. Flywheel purpose

        2. Pistons and rods

            a. Offset
            b. Assembly markings
            c. Spit-hole

3. Rings

    a. Compression
    b. Scraper
    c. Oil (3 piece)
    d. Materials
    e. Top-side markings

4. Cylinder head

D. Valve Train

1. Camshaft

    a. What speed in relation to crankshaft?
    b. Lift
    c. Duration
    d. Location
    e. Lobe profile nomenclature

2. Hydraulic valve lifters

    a. Advantages
    b. Operation
    c. Adjustment

3. Cam drive methods

    a. Gears
    b. Chain and sprockets
    c. Belt

4. Push rods
5. Rocker arms

    a. Geometry

6. Valves

    a. Intake
    b. Exhaust
    c. Stem seals
    d. Keepers
    e. Retainers and springs
    f. Rotators
    g. Guides

E.  Lubrication System

    1. API oil classifications
    2. Types of oil pumps

        a. Required clearances
        b. Where are clearances checked?
        c. Oil pump wear

    3. By-pass and full-flow system

        a. Oil filters

    4. Oil pressure light operation
    5. Pre-lubricating engine oiling system prior to starting
    6. Bearings

        a. Rod
        b. Main
        c. Thrust type
        d. Cam
        e. Purpose of crush and spread
        f. Plastigage
        g. Operating clearances

F.  Cooling System

    1. Water circulation flow
    2. Radiator design

        a. Crossflow
        b. Downflow

    3. System deposits

        a. Electrolysis

    4. Flushing
    5. Water pumps

        a. Aeration
        b. By-pass

    6. Radiator pressure caps

        a. Collapsed hose

7. Temperature control

    a. Thermostats
    b. Viscous fans
    c. Shrouds

8. Drive belts

    a. Glaze
    b. Fraying
    c. Methods of adjustment

G. Intake Manifold System

1. Improper torque could result in?
2. Runner layout design
3. Heat cross-over
4. Warpage

H. Exhaust System

1. Collapsed exhaust pipe
2. Manifold heat control valve

II. Engine Service Procedures (Emphasis is Placed on the Type and Use of Tools)

A. Be Able to Identify Visually

  1. Micrometers
  2. Cylinder bore gauges
  3. Cylinder hones
  4. Torque wrenches (click, beam, and dial types)
  5. Electromagnetic crack detection equipment
  6. Checking warpage with a straightedge and feeler gauge
  7. Dial indicator checks
  8. Hydraulic lifter leak-down test fixture
  9. Ridge reamers
10. Rod alignment fixture
11. Ring groove cleaning tool
12. Cooling system pressure tester
13. Valve seat concentricity gauge

B. Block Assembly

1. Crankshaft measurements

    a. Taper
    b. Out-of-round
    c. End-play
    d. Run-out

    2. Cylinder measurements

        a. Taper
        b. Out-of-round

    3. Camshaft measurements

        a. T.I.R. (total indicated run-out)
        b. Lift
        c. Base circle run-out
        d. End-play

    4. Main bearing bore measurement

        a. Out-of-round
        b. Alignment

C. Heads and Valves

    1. Valve and seat refacing

        a. Margin
        b. Seat width and location
        c. Interference angles
        d. "Throating" and "topping"
        e. Concentricity checks

    2. Valve guide measurement
    3. Valve guide reconditioning
    4. Head surfacing

        a. Correct tightening sequence

    5. Valve spring measurements

        a. Shims

    6. Valve tip height

D. Piston and Rings

    1. Piston design
    2. Piston measurements

        a. Knurling

    3. Ring installation

        a. End-gap measurement and position
        b. Ring side clearance
        c. Ring depth

4. Cylinder wall reconditioning

   a. Washing with soap and water

5. Piston ring groove wear

   a. Groove inserts

E. Rods, Pins, and Bearings

   1. Rod alignment

      a. Checking piston skirt wear pattern
      b. Big-end wear

   2. Piston pin types
   3. Rod bearing measurements
   4. Rod bearing service

III. Engine Problem/Diagnosis

A. Noises

   1. Piston slap
   2. Piston pin
   3. Rod bearings

      a. Wear analysis

   4. Main bearings

      a. Wear analysis

   5. Crankshaft thrust
   6. Valves

      a. Lifters
      b. Rocker arms
      c. Wear analysis

   7. Ring click
   8. Flywheel knock

B. Oil Consumption

   1. Rings
   2. Valves
   3. Guides
   4. Leaks

      a. Black-light detection

   5. Defective intake manifold gaskets

C.  Water Consumption

  1.  Internal
  2.  External

D.  Low Oil Pressure

  1.  Worn cam bearings

E.  Low Compression

  1.  Test procedures

F.  Interpretation of Vacuum Gauge Readings
G.  Worn Timing Chain Assembly

---

EXERCISES

1.  Starting with the micrometer's spindle down against the anvil,
    how many complete turns of the thimble will it take to move the
    spindle away from the anvil exactly one inch?

    a.  25
    b.  40
    c.  50
    d.  100

2.  The decimal equivalent of 7/16 of an inch is:

    a.  .4219
    b.  .3750
    c.  .4375
    d.  .4531

3.  "Cam" ground pistons, as they warm up, take on:

    a.  An oval shape
    b.  A round shape
    c.  Additional eccentricity to improve oil clearance
    d.  A tapered shape

4. How much will the coolant boiling point be raised if a 13-pound
   cap is installed on a radiator?


   a. 13°F
   b. 26°F
   c. 39°F
   d. 65°F


5. What is the cubic inch displacement of a V-8 engine that has a
   4-inch bore with a 4-inch stroke?


   a. 350 cubic inches
   b. 390 cubic inches
   c. 402 cubic inches
   d. 454 cubic inches


6. You are rebuilding a small block Chevrolet engine and find a heavy
   build-up of hard carbon on the fillet radius of each intake valve.
   What would you suspect?


   a. Poor valve seating
   b. Tapered cylinder walls
   c. Excessive valve guide clearance
   d. Stuck oil control rings


7. Mechanic A says that exhaust valve burning may be caused by an overly
   rich air-fuel mixture.

   Mechanic B says that a defective thermostat can cause exhaust valve
   burning.

   Who is right?


   a. Mechanic A
   b. Mechanic B
   c. Both A and B
   d. Neither A nor B

8. The camshaft for a typical OHV V-8 engine has:

   a. 8 lobes
   b. 4 lobes
   c. 16 lobes
   d. 32 lobes

←16" LEVER LENGTH OF WRENCH→

FOOT POUND SCALE

9. You have to use an adapter that adds four inches to the length of
   the above torque wrench.  What should the dial read if you want to
   tighten a bolt to 30 ft. lbs.?

   a. 18 ft. lbs.
   b. 24 ft. lbs.
   c. 28 ft. lbs.
   d. 40 ft. lbs.

10. Mechanic A says that plastigage becomes wider as clearance increases.

    Mechanic B says that plastigage becomes narrower as clearance
    decreases.

    Who is right?

    a. Mechanic A
    b. Mechanic B
    c. Both A and B
    d. Neither A nor B

11. Connecting rod number markings are usually stamped on a V-8 engine
    by the factory:

    a. On the side of the rod that is closest to the camshaft
    b. On the side of the rod away from the camshaft
    c. On the beam of the rod facing the front of the engine
    d. On the bottom of the rod cap

12. You are replacing rod bearings on an engine.  The crankpin diameter
    measures 2.016".  Standard crankpin diameter measures 2.046".  What
    size bearings would you order from parts?


    a. U/S - .015
    b. U/S - .030
    c. Standard size
    d. O/S - .030


13. When installing a new set of piston rings, you discover that all
    the top compression rings have a side clearance varying from .012"
    to .018".  What would you do?


    a. Install ring expanders.
    b. Increase the ring groove width.
    c. Replace the pistons.
    d. Nothing--this is an acceptable specification.

14. What would be the major problem if the part (shown above) were
    left out when rebuilding a typical V-8 engine?


    a. The engine would have no oil pressure.
    b. In the event of a clogged oil filter, there would be no by-pass.
    c. The engine would have excessively high oil pressure.
    d. The camshaft would have excessive end thrust.


15. You are doing the second valve job on an engine.  You are grinding
    the seats, and replacing all the valves and springs.  Which measure-
    ment will have to be corrected back to specification?


    a. Free length
    b. Margin width
    c. Installed height
    d. Throat angle

FRONT OF ENGINE

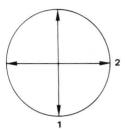

16. You are "miking" cylinder diameter on an engine with 90,000 miles. The greatest diameter will occur at the _____ of the cylinder in direction __.

   a. Top, #1
   b. Top, #2
   c. Middle, #1
   d. Middle, #2

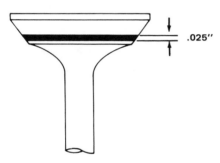

.025″

17. You are assembling a cylinder head after someone else has ground the valves and seats. You discover that several exhaust valves have seat contact as shown above. What needs to be done to correct this situation?

   a. Grind the seat with a 45° stone, and then narrow with a 60° cutter.
   b. Widen the seat with a 45° stone.
   c. Grind the seat with a 45° stone, and then widen with a 15° cutter.
   d. Widen the seat with a 30° stone.

18. The above pattern is observed on the skirt of a piston.  What is
    indicated?


    a. A twisted rod
    b. A collapsed piston
    c. An out-of-round bushing
    d. The piston was installed with the off-set to the wrong side of the rod.

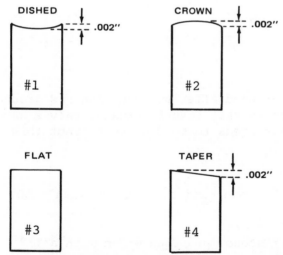

19. You are installing a set of new hydraulic valve lifters in an engine.
    What should be the shape of the new lifter bottom (see above)?


    a. Illustration #1
    b. Illustration #2
    c. Illustration #3
    d. Illustration #4

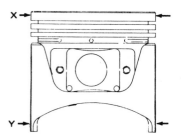

20. Refer to the picture above.

Mechanic A says that piston diameter measurement is generally made across point X.

Mechanic B says that piston diameter measurement is generally made across point Y.

Who is right?


   a. Mechanic A
   b. Mechanic B
   c. Either A or B
   d. Neither A nor B


21. You are doing a ring job on an engine.  The cylinders have .015" taper.  Which of the following would be correct procedure?


   a. Bore the engine.
   b. Install expanders behind the new rings.
   c. Knurl the pistons.
   d. None of the above--this is an acceptable taper specification.


22. A worn and stretched timing chain will:


   a. Retard valve timing
   b. Advance valve timing
   c. Either retard or advance valve timing depending on engine speed
   d. Either retard or advance valve timing depending on engine load


23. When reinstalling a cylinder head, the torquing sequence would start:


   a. At the ends
   b. In the middle
   c. At the #1 cylinder
   d. At the side next to the exhaust manifold

24. A "cam" ground type piston will have its largest diameter:

    a. Across the skirt parallel to the pin
    b. At 45° from the pin centerline
    c. Across the thrust face 90° from the pin
    d. At 45° from the pin bosses

25. An engine with a cylinder bore of 3-13/16" is bored eighty-thousandths oversize. What will the new diameter be?

    a. 3.8205"
    b. 3.8650"
    c. 3.8750"
    d. 3.8925"

26. When installing a camshaft, you accidentally knock out the block plug at the rear. What would result when the engine was started?

    a. Engine coolant would get into the oil.
    b. An oil pressure loss would occur.
    c. Both a and b
    d. Neither a nor b

27. "Topping" a valve seat (45° angle) would most likely be accomplished with a:

    a. 15° stone
    b. 30° stone
    c. 45° stone
    d. 60° stone

28. Normal piston ring end gap clearance in automotive engines with conventional cast iron or chrome rings is _____ per inch of bore diameter.

    a. .0005 - .0015"
    b. .003 - .004"
    c. .007 - .009"
    d. .012 - .016"

29. An automobile engine block is going to be reverse flushed. The
radiator has been removed for service. The radiator hoses have
been left attached to the engine.

Mechanic A says to install the flushing gun into the lower radiator
hose.

Mechanic B says to install the flushing gun into the water pump
by-pass hose.

Who is right?


a. Mechanic A
b. Mechanic B
c. Either A or B
d. Neither A nor B


30. A customer complains of the following problem with his car: The
engine develops severe hydraulic valve lifter noise after a few
miles of driving. This occurs only at speeds above 40 mph.

Mechanic A says that too much oil in the crankcase could be the
problem.

Mechanic B says that a crack in the oil pump pick-up tube could
be the problem.

Who is right?


a. Mechanic A
b. Mechanic B
c. Either A or B
d. Neither A nor B

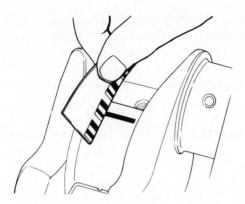

31. What is the mechanic doing in the picture above?


    a. Determining main bearing clearance
    b. Determining rod bearing clearance
    c. Measuring crankshaft end-play
    d. Measuring journal out-of-roundness


32. How many revolutions does the crankshaft have to make in order for
    all the cylinders to fire in a four stroke cycle V-8 engine?


    a. 16
    b. 8
    c. 4
    d. 2


33. A customer is having the third new water pump installed on his car.
    The two previous pumps failed (the shaft fractured) within a few
    thousand miles of driving.  What could be causing this problem?


    a. A defective viscous fan clutch assembly
    b. An over-tightened belt
    c. A bent fan blade
    d. Any of the above

34. A light double knocking noise is heard from an idling engine.

    Mechanic A says that it could be worn rod bearings.

    Mechanic B says that it could be worn piston pins.

    Who is right?


    a. Mechanic A
    b. Mechanic B
    c. Either A or B
    d. Neither A nor B


FIG 1                    FIG 2

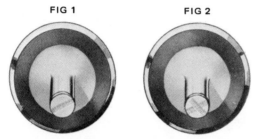

35. An engine is equipped with valve rotators.  Which wear pattern above
    would indicate that the rotator is functioning properly?


    a. Figure 1
    b. Figure 2
    c. Either Figure 1 or Figure 2
    d. Neither Figure 1 nor Figure 2


36. Two mechanics are having a discussion about doing a valve job.

    Mechanic A says to knurl the valve guides before grinding the seats.

    Mechanic B says to grind the valve seats first.

    Who is right?


    a. Mechanic A
    b. Mechanic B
    c. Either A or B
    d. Neither A nor B

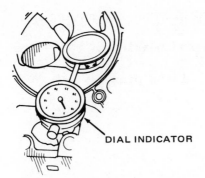

DIAL INDICATOR

37. Refer to the above illustration.  What is the mechanic measuring?

   a. Valve guide wear
   b. Valve margin
   c. Valve lift
   d. Valve face concentricity

38. A typical interference angle would find the valve faced at an angle:

   a. 4° less than the seat angle
   b. 2° less than the seat angle
   c. 1° less than the seat angle
   d. 1° greater than the seat angle

39. You are doing a valve job.  The valve springs should be checked for:

   a. Squareness
   b. Installed height
   c. Tension
   d. All of the above

40. You are assembling a typical 6-cylinder engine.  In what direction
    should the rocker shaft oil feed holes face?

   a. Downward
   b. Upward
   c. Toward the push rods
   d. Opposite the push rods

41. The illustration above shows the bearing shell to have some additional
    height over a full half.  This is done to provide for:


    a. Spread
    b. Crush
    c. An adjustment
    d. Embedability


42. You are replacing a radiator hose (for the third time in a month)
    that is torn.  What could be the possible cause?


    a. A loose mounted radiator
    b. A loose radiator shroud
    c. A defective radiator cap
    d. Damaged motor mount(s)


43. A customer drives his vehicle into a shop.  He wants to know why
    the upper radiator hose collapses as the engine cools off.

    Mechanic A says that this is caused by a defective thermostat.

    Mechanic B says that the cause is a loose hose clamp connection.

    Who is right?


    a. Mechanic A
    b. Mechanic B
    c. Either A or B
    d. Neither A nor B

44. Mechanic A says that a cracked cylinder head can cause ethylene glycol to seep into the oil.

    Mechanic B says that a cracked cylinder head can cause engine overheating.

    Who is right?

    a. Mechanic A
    b. Mechanic B
    c. Both A and B
    d. Neither A nor B

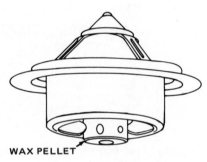

WAX PELLET

45. You are installing the above thermostat.  The pellet end of the thermostat must be installed:

    a. Toward the engine
    b. Toward the radiator
    c. In the manifold tee
    d. In the by-pass hose

GAUGE

46. You pressurize a cooling system with the tester shown above.  Which
    of the following is an indication of a leak?


    a. The gauge pressure drops quickly.
    b. The gauge pressure stays the same for one minute and then
       starts to drop slowly.
    c. The gauge pressure slowly goes up.
    d. None of the above.


47. You are rebuilding a typical V-8 engine.  The most normal main
    bearing clearance specification would be:


    a. .300"
    b. .030"
    c. .003"
    d. .0003"


48. After honing or deglazing, cylinder walls should be washed with:


    a. Oil soaked rags
    b. Soap and water
    c. Kerosene
    d. Cleaning solvent

49. An engine has been recently overhauled. At 5000 rpm a piston pin
    lock ring snaps out of position, and severe cylinder wall damage
    results. What could have caused this failure?

    a. Overstressing the lock ring during installation
    b. Installing the lock ring with the open end facing up
    c. A piston lock ring groove that was too shallow
    d. Any of the above

50. You are going to install new piston rings in an engine. If the
    ring ridge is not removed:

    a. The piston will be hard to install.
    b. The cylinder walls will be distorted.
    c. The top ring and piston land can be broken.
    d. The rings will not seat properly.

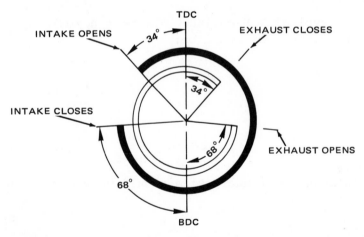

51. Refer to the valve timing diagram above. The intake valve is off
    its seat for how many degress of crankshaft rotation?

    a. 68°
    b. 102°
    c. 248°
    d. 282°

52. A mechanic has just completed a valve job on a V-8 engine that is equipped with nonadjustable hydraulic lifters. He cannot start the engine. A compression test is made, and six cylinders read zero. What should be done?

   a. Install two head gaskets on each bank.
   b. Grind material off the bottom of each rocker stand.
   c. Grind the valve tips.
   d. Install longer push rods.

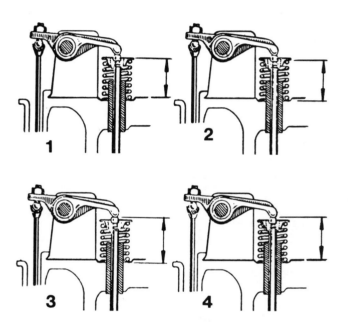

53. Which illustration above shows the correct dimension points for measuring installed valve spring height?

   a. 1
   b. 2
   c. 3
   d. 4

54. Which of the measurements below is not within specifications on a
    typical engine?

    a. Valve-stem-to-guide clearance - .002"
    b. Cylinder head warpage - .004"
    c. Intake valve seat width - .125"
    d. Exhaust valve margin - 1/32"

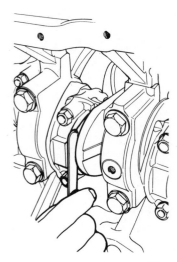

55. What is the mechanic doing in the picture above?

    a. Measuring crankshaft thrust play
    b. Measuring connecting rod side clearance
    c. Checking the fillet radius
    d. Checking the oil clearance

56. You are about to assemble a cylinder head.  You notice that the valve
    springs have the coils closer together at one end.  How should the
    springs be installed?

    Mechanic A says that the closed coil end of the spring should go toward
    the head of the valve.

    Mechanic B says that the closed coil end goes toward the valve tip.

    Who is right?

    a. Mechanic A
    b. Mechanic B
    c. Either A or B
    d. Neither A nor B

57. Exhaust valve lash (with cast iron heads) is generally set wider than intake valve lash.

   Mechanic A says that this is necessary because of valve overlap.

   Mechanic B says this is because exhaust valves run hotter and expand more than intake valves.

   Who is right?

   a. Mechanic A
   b. Mechanic B
   c. Both A and B
   d. Neither A nor B

58. Mechanic A says that cylinder wear is greatest at the bottom of ring travel.

   Mechanic B says that cylinder wear is greatest at the center of ring travel.

   Who is right?

   a. Mechanic A
   b. Mechanic B
   c. Both A and B
   d. Neither A nor B

59. Crankshaft main journals and rod crankpins are measured and checked for:

   a. Out-of-round
   b. Taper
   c. Diameter
   d. All of the above

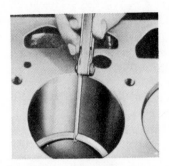

60. What measurement check is the mechanic performing in the picture above?

   a. Piston clearance
   b. Cylinder out-of-round
   c. Cylinder taper
   d. Piston ring end gap

61. A car owner says that the dashboard oil pressure light flickers on and off while the engine is idling.

    Mechanic A says that a weak pressure relief valve spring in the oil pump could be the cause.

    Mechanic B says that worn crankshaft bearings could be the cause.

    Who is right?

   a. Mechanic A
   b. Mechanic B
   c. Either A or B
   d. Neither A nor B

62. Which of the following can cause low oil pressure?

   a. Worn cam bearings
   b. Excessive rod bearing clearance
   c. Excessive main bearing clearance
   d. All of the above

63. You make a compression test and obtain a low reading in two adjacent cylinders.  This would most likely indicate:

    a. A leaking intake manifold gasket
    b. A leaking exhaust manifold gasket
    c. A leaking cylinder head gasket
    d. A burned valve

64. A vehicle is towed into a shop with a ruptured oil filter.

    Mechanic A says that this often happens when the filter in a full-flow system clogs up.

    Mechanic B says that pieces of nylon from a worn timing gear may have entered into the pressure relief valve of the oil pump, causing extreme high pressure.

    Who is right?

    a. Mechanic A
    b. Mechanic B
    c. Both A and B
    d. Neither A nor B

65. A cylinder head is being measured for warpage using a straightedge and feeler gauge.

    Mechanic A says to measure diagonally from corner to corner.

    Mechanic B says to measure across the center of the head.

    Who is right?

    a. Mechanic A
    b. Mechanic B
    c. Both A and B
    d. Neither A nor B

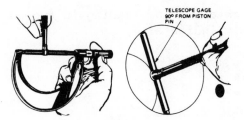

66. Refer to the above instruments.  What is being measured?


    a. Cylinder bore diameter
    b. Piston diameter
    c. Both a and b
    d. Neither a nor b

67. What does the bearing wear pattern shown above indicate?


    a. Saddle bores out of line
    b. Fatigue failure
    c. Radius ride
    d. Insufficient lubrication

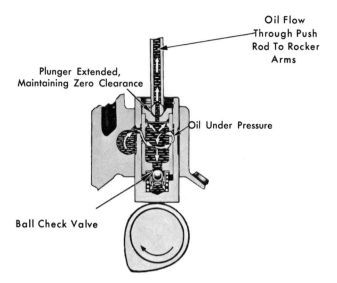

Oil Flow Through Push Rod To Rocker Arms

Plunger Extended, Maintaining Zero Clearance

Oil Under Pressure

Ball Check Valve

68. Refer to the valve lifter mechanism shown above.

Mechanic A says that slight leakage should now be occurring between the plunger and lifter body.

Mechanic B says that leakage is designed to occur when the ball check valve is closed.

Who is right?


a. Mechanic A
b. Mechanic B
c. Both A and B
d. Neither A nor B


69 Mechanic A says that the oil control ring has oil return slots or holes.

Mechanic B says that on a three-ring piston, the oil control ring is installed in the bottom groove.

Who is right?


a. Mechanic A
b. Mechanic B
c. Both A and B
d. Neither A nor B

70. What are the two major places through which the exhaust valve dissipates its heat?

    a. Valve spring retainer and spring
    b. Valve guide and valve lifter
    c. Valve guide and valve seat
    d. Valve guide and rocker arm

71. The cylinders on an engine have .007" taper. If the cylinders are rigid honed to remove the taper, the pistons:

    a. Will require resizing
    b. Will require the installation of top ring groove inserts
    c. Should be discarded and new pistons installed
    d. Both a and b above

72. Mechanic A says that excessive crankcase blow-by can be caused by worn piston rings.

Mechanic B says that a collapsed piston can cause excessive crankcase blow-by.

Who is right?

    a. Mechanic A
    b. Mechanic B
    c. Both A and B
    d. Neither A nor B

PLATFORM KNOB

73. Refer to the test being performed above.

Mechanic A says that the platform knob must be set to the compressed length of the spring.

Mechanic B says to apply torque until a click is heard, then read the torque wrench and multiply the reading by 2.

Who is right?

a. Mechanic A
b. Mechanic B
c. Both A and B
d. Neither A nor B

74. A cooling system thermostat rated at 180°F will:

a. Start to open at 177° to 182°F
b. Be fully open at 177° to 182°F
c. Start to open at 160°F
d. Be fully open at 180°F

75. A V-8 engine (firing order 18436572) has been turned to the No. 1 firing position.  What valves may now be adjusted?

a. Exhaust valves 1, 3, 4, and 8
b. Intake valves 1, 2, 5, and 7
c. Both a and b
d. Neither a nor b

76. Which of the following can cause rust to form in the cooling system?


    a. A lower radiator hose clamp that is not tight
    b. A slight water pump leak
    c. A defective head gasket
    d. All of the above

# 4

# ENGINE TUNE-UP

STUDY OUTLINE

I. Fuel and Induction System

   A. Intake Manifolds

      1. Runner configuration (fuel distribution)
      2. Exhaust crossover
      3. Vacuum leak areas
      4. Bolt torque tightening pattern
      5. Poor gasket seating

   B. Fuel Supply System

      1. Fuel tank and safety cap
      2. Filters
      3. Lines and hoses
      4. Fuel pumps
      5. Service procedures

   C. Carburetor Circuits (Understand Principles of Operation)

      1. Float
      2. Idle and low-speed
      3. Main metering
      4. Pump
      5. Power (enrichment)
      6. Automatic choke
      7. Identify typical components from each circuit above

   D. Crankcase Ventilation System

      1. PCV valve
      2. Type 1
      3. Type 3
      4. Type 4
      5. Testing/Servicing
      6. Problem/Diagnosis

         a. Stuck open
         b. Stuck closed

E.  Air Cleaners

1.  Types
2.  Servicing


II.  Fuel and Induction System Problem/Diagnosis

A.  Fuel Pumps

1.  Typical specifications
2.  Pressure testing
3.  Vacuum testing
4.  Volume test
5.  Porous diaphragm (oil consumption)
6.  Noise

B.  Carburetor

1.  Flooding
2.  Hard cold starting
3.  Hard hot starting
4.  Hesitation (off-idle)
5.  Surging
6.  Poor mileage
7.  Rough idle
8.  Loss of power
9.  Flat-spot when accelerating
10.  Vacuum leaks
11.  Plugged air bleeds
12.  Misaligned throttle plates
13.  Defective choke break diaphragm
14.  Defective antipercolator valve
15.  Dieseling
16.  Black smoke from exhaust pipe during idle
17.  Engine will not idle below 1500 rpm

C.  Carburetor Adjustments (Effects if Not Correct)

1.  Float level and float drop
2.  Unloader
3.  Fast idle setting
4.  Curb idle setting
5.  Choke plate pull-off
6.  Idle mixture (limiters)
7.  Pump stroke
8.  Secondary lock-out
9.  Idle solenoid settings
10.  Choke plate tension

D. Know the Typical Procedure for Making Each of the Preceding Adjustments

E. Carburetor Cleaning Procedures

III. Exhaust System

A. Manifold Heat Control Valve Operation
B. Heated Air Intake System Ducting
C. Choke

1. Exhaust gas heated air
2. Hot water
3. Electric (stator current)

IV. Exhaust System Problem/Diagnosis

A. Leaks
B. Collapsed Pipe (Restricted on the Inside)

1. Testing with a vacuum gauge

C. Manifold Heat Control Valve Stuck

1. Open
2. Closed
3. Lubrication
4. Replacement procedure

V. Ignition System

A. Primary (Low Voltage)

1. Battery
2. Ignition switch
3. Ballast resistor or resistance wire
4. Coil primary winding
5. Condenser
6. Points
7. Harness wiring
8. System grounds

B.  Secondary (High Voltage)

1. Coil secondary winding
2. Distributor cap
3. Rotor
4. Spark plug wiring
5. Plugs
6. System grounds

C.  Distributor Spark Timing Mechanisms

1. Retard and advance diaphragms
2. Centrifugal weight assembly
3. Theory of operation
4. Adjusting timing
5. Initial timing
6. Total advance

VI.  Ignition System Problems/Diagnosis

A.  Engine Missing

1. At idle
2. Under load
3. Spark plug condition
4. Incorrect timing
5. Point alignment
6. Point wear

B.  Engine Cranks But Will Not Start
C.  Engine Backfires

1. Spark plug wire routing
2. Carbon tracking

D.  Engine Lacks Power
E.  Engine Starts During Crank but Quits When Key is Released to Run Position

F.  Spark Timing Problems

1. Breaker plate wear
2. Cam wear
3. Bent distributor shaft
4. Sticking weights
5. Incorrect vacuum diaphragm hose hook-up

G. Engine Difficult to Start When Cold
H. Engine Difficult to Start When Hot
I. Excessive Voltage Drop in the Primary Circuit

VII. Use of Test Equipment (Adjustments or Service to Bring Vehicle to Specification)

A. Voltmeter
B. Ammeter
C. Ohmmeter
D. Compression Gauge
E. Cylinder Leakage Test
F. Cylinder Balance
G. Distributor Strobe Machine
H. Oscilloscope

1. Basic patterns (know the sections)

a. Primary
b. Secondary
c. Superimposed
d. Parade
e. Raster

2. Diagnostic Tests/Pattern Interpretation

a. Reversed polarity
b. Coil output
c. Ignition reserve
d. Rotor gap KV requirement
e. Point misalignment
f. Shorted coil
g. Secondary insulation
h. Worn distributor shaft bushings
i. Open plug wire
j. Fouled plug
k. Lean mixture
l. Coil tower corrosion
m. Spark line slopes upward
n. Spark line slopes downward
o. Point resistance
p. Dwell variation

I. Tach/Dwell Meter

J.  Infrared Analyzer

    1. Meter interpretation

        a. High HC
        b. High CO
        c. Low CO
        d. Fluctuating HC reading

    2. Know typical causes for each of the above readings
    3. 2500 rpm test

K.  Interpretation of Vacuum Gauge Readings

VIII.  Basic Emission Control Systems (The Test Does Not Emphasize Makes
      or Models; Be Concerned with Principles of Operation)

A.  Crankcase Ventilation Devices

    1. See section I-D

B.  Combustion Controls (For Hydrocarbon Control)

    1. Air injection (AIR)
    2. Improved combustion (IMPCO)
    3. Clean air systems (CAS)
    4. Testing/Servicing

        a. Air pump
        b. Relief valve
        c. Check valve
        d. Diverter or gulp valve
        e. Air manifold
        f. Vacuum advance control valves

C.  Vapor Control Systems

    1. Crankcase storage
    2. Carbon cannister storage
    3. Vapor separator
    4. Check valves
    5. Tank caps
    6. Air cleaner connections
    7. Testing/Service
    8. Problem/Diagnosis

        a. Liquid gas in carbon cannister
        b. Collapsed tank

D.  Temperature Controlled Air Cleaner

    1. Vacuum motor
    2. Air door
    3. Temperature sensor
    4. Testing/Service
    5. Problem/Diagnosis

        a. Effects of vacuum loss
        b. Vacuum motor defects
        c. Temperature sensor defects
        d. Stuck air door

E.  Exhaust Gas Recirculating System (EGR)

    1. For $NO_x$ control
    2. Vacuum operated
    3. EGR valve diaphragm
    4. Floor jets
    5. Testing/Service
    6. Problem/Diagnosis

        a. Rough idle
        b. No EGR valve stem movement

F.  Distributor Advance Control Systems

    1. See section V-C
    2. For $NO_x$ control
    3. Vacuum retard
    4. Electric retard
    5. Transmission controlled spark (TCS)
    6. Thermal controls
    7. Speed controls
    8. Testing/Service
    9. Problem/Diagnosis

        a. Engine overheating

G.  Catalytic Converter System

    1. Components
    2. Converter construction
    3. Testing/Service
    4. Problem/Diagnosis

        a. Converter overheating
        b. Effects of using leaded gas
        c. Don't remove plug wires when engine is running
        d. "Rotten egg" exhaust gas smell
        e. Infrared service tap in front of converter

EXERCISES

1. Mechanic A says that ignition timing should be adjusted before
   adjusting the points.

   Mechanic B says that ignition timing is adjusted either before or
   after adjusting the points.

   Who is right?


   a. Mechanic A
   b. Mechanic B
   c. Either A or B
   d. Neither A nor B


2. On a vehicle with a conventional battery ignition system, maximum
   coil output should be:


   a. Less than 20 KV
   b. 20 KV or more
   c. 50 KV or more
   d. 100 KV or more

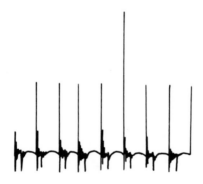

3. The oscilloscope pattern above indicates what problem?


   a. A defective coil
   b. A defective condenser
   c. Point bounce
   d. An open spark plug wire

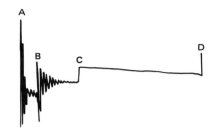

4. Refer to the pattern above. Which letter indicates where the ignition points close?

    a. A
    b. B
    c. C
    d. D

5. You are checking ignition coil available voltage with an oscilloscope. What is the procedure?

    a. Remove a plug wire at the spark plug and ground it.
    b. Remove a plug wire at the spark plug and hold it away from ground.
    c. Remove the coil wire and ground it on the engine block.
    d. Remove the primary coil wire and ground it on the engine block.

6. Mechanic A says that distributor vacuum diaphragms are used to retard spark timing.

    Mechanic B says that distributor vacuum diaphragms are used to advance spark timing.

    Who is right?

    a. Mechanic A
    b. Mechanic B
    c. Both A and B
    d. Neither A nor B

7. Which figure below would be a typical charging circuit voltage reading for a 12-volt system?

   a. 13.8 to 14.8 volts
   b. 14.9 to 16.1 volts
   c. 11.5 to 13.3 volts
   d. 7.5 to 8.4 volts

8. An engine starts with the key switch in the "crank" position. When the switch is released to the "run" position, the engine dies. What is the most likely cause of this problem?

   a. A defective ignition resistor
   b. A defective coil
   c. A defective starter solenoid
   d. A defective neutral switch

9. Point gap set wider than specification would result in:

   a. Retarded spark timing
   b. Reduced dwell
   c. Both a and b
   d. Neither a nor b

10. An engine is operating at 3000 rpm. The distributor is turning at:

   a. 6000 rpm
   b. 3000 rpm
   c. 1500 rpm
   d. 4500 rpm

11. The dwell has changed from 30° to 31° because of rubbing block wear. What is the change on the spark timing?

   a. A 1° retard change
   b. A 2° advance change
   c. A 2° retard change
   d. A 1/2° advance change

12. Mechanic A says cam angle (dwell) is the number of degrees of distributor cam rotation during which the points are open.

   Mechanic B says that cam angle is the angle at which the rubbing makes contact with the distributor cam.

   Who is right?

   a. Mechanic A
   b. Mechanic B
   c. Both A and B
   d. Neither A nor B

13. Most carburetors have a constriction in the main body section called the venturi.

   Mechanic A says that the venturi causes a decrease in air velocity at the fuel nozzle.

   Mechanic B says that the venturi causes a decrease in pressure at the fuel nozzle.

   Who is right?

   a. Mechanic A
   b. Mechanic B
   c. Both A and B
   d. Neither A nor B

14. The three times that the engine generally requires the richest air-fuel mixture is during:

   a. Starting, idling, and full throttle operation
   b. Starting, acceleration, and full throttle operation
   c. Starting, part throttle, and full throttle operation
   d. Hot weather, high altitude, and high speed operation

15. Mechanic A says that an accelerating pump is used in carburetors because the fuel pump can't supply fuel rapidly enough when the throttle is suddenly opened.

    Mechanic B says that it is used because the mixture gets leaner when the throttle is opened suddenly.

    Who is right?

    a. Mechanic A
    b. Mechanic B
    c. Both A and B
    d. Neither A nor B

16. The choke thermostatic coil spring tends to _____ the choke plate, and the choke vacuum diaphragm tends to _____ the choke plate.

    a. Open, close
    b. Close, open
    c. Close, close
    d. Open, open

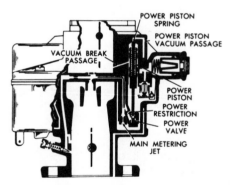

17. The above carburetor is being used on an engine.  When engine load is increased the power piston is moved ____ by _____ to _____ the power valve.

    a. Down, spring tension, open
    b. Up, vacuum, open
    c. Down, vacuum, open
    d. Up, spring tension, close

18. Fast idling of the engine when it is cold is generally obtained by
    means of:


    a. A fast idle circuit in the carburetor
    b. A fast idle cam
    c. An electro-vacuum switch
    d. A valve in the carburetor


19. Two mechanics are having a discussion about carburetors with
    automatic chokes.

    Mechanic A says that some carburetors are designed to have hot
    water (radiator coolant) going to the thermostatic coil housing.

    Mechanic B says that some carburetors are designed to have exhaust
    gas going into the thermostatic coil housing.

    Who is right?


    a. Mechanic A
    b. Mechanic B
    c. Both A and B
    d. Neither A nor B


20. Setting the carburetor float level lower than factory specification
    could cause:


    a. Too lean a mixture
    b. "Surge" at cruising speeds
    c. Both a and b
    d. Neither a nor b

TO CARBURETOR

21. The thermostatically controlled air cleaner shown above:


    a. Is providing heated air to the carb
    b. Has the hot air passage open
    c. Both a and b
    d. Neither a nor b

22. A carburetor is being repaired because of a malfunctioning automatic
    choke.  The choke housing is corroded inside and there are heavy
    carbon accumulations on the choke piston.

    Mechanic A says to replace the carburetor.

    Mechanic B says to check the manifold heat pipe for leaks.

    Who is right?


    a. Mechanic A
    b. Mechanic B
    c. Both A and B
    d. Neither A nor B


23. A carburetor has an economizer valve that is leaking slightly.
    How would this be indicated on an infrared analyzer?


    a. High HC
    b. High HC and low CO
    c. High CO
    d. The HC meter needle will fluctuate

                    ─── AIR GAP

24. To set the air gap on the electronic ignition system shown above, the
    mechanic would use:


    a. A special design dwell meter
    b. A brass feeler gauge
    c. A self-powered test lamp
    d. An ohmmeter

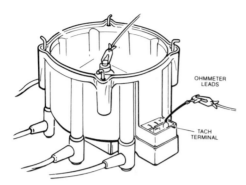

25. A high energy ignition system (HEI) is being checked.  What
    test is being performed above?


    a. Ballast resistance
    b. Ignition coil primary
    c. Ignition coil secondary
    d. None of the above

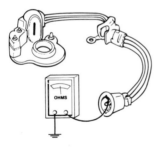

26. What electronic ignition system component is being tested in the
    above drawing?


    a. The reluctor
    b. The trigger wheel
    c. The magnetic pickup assembly
    d. The compensating resistor

27. An engine is idling in the shop.  A mechanic pulls the PCV valve
    out of the valve cover and puts his finger over the opening.  There
    is no change in engine rpm.

    Mechanic A says that the hose between the intake manifold and PCV
    valve could be plugged up.

    Mechanic B says that the PCV valve could be stuck open.

    Who is right?


    A. Mechanic A
    b. Mechanic B
    c. Both A and B
    d. Neither A nor B


28. You are about to adjust valve lash on an overhead cam engine
    equipped with solid lifters.

    Mechanic A says that not enough lash can cause the valves to burn.

    Mechanic B says that too much lash can cause noise and poor engine
    performance.

    Who is right?


    a. Mechanic A
    b. Mechanic B
    d. Either A or B
    d. Neither A nor B

29. The part above is stuck in the open position.

Mechanic A says that this could cause poor gas mileage.

Mechanic B says that this could cause lower intake manifold vacuum,
and result in overheating.

Who is right?


a. Mechanic A
b. Mechanic B
c. Both A and B
d. Neither A nor B

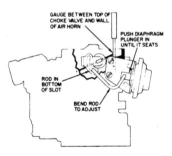

30. Refer to the drawing above.   What adjustment is being checked?


a. Choke plate lockout
b. Dashpot
c. Unloader
d. Vacuum break

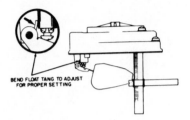

31. The drawing above shows what carburetor adjustment?


    a. Float level
    b. Float drop
    c. Float alignment
    d. None of the above

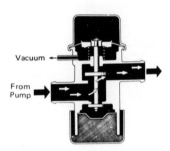

32. The above pictured valve is used on a vehicle with an AIR system.

    Mechanic A says that the purpose of the valve is to enrich the air-
    fuel mixture on deceleration.

    Mechanic B says that the purpose of the valve is to prevent back-
    fire.

    Who is right?


    a. Mechanic A
    b. Mechanic B
    c. Both A and B
    d. Neither A nor B

33. What is the firing order on most 6 cylinder in-line engines?

    a. 1, 3, 5, 6, 2, 4
    b. 1, 6, 5, 4, 3, 2
    c. 1, 5, 3, 6, 2, 4
    d. 1, 5, 3, 2, 6, 4

34. Metering rods (used on some carburetors) are designed to vary the size of which jets?

    a. Idle jets
    b. Acceleration jets
    c. Main jets
    d. Floor jets

35. The cause of a line of black sooty deposits under the distributor contact points could be:

    a. Excessive cam lubricant
    b. Crankcase pressurization
    c. A plugged PCV system
    d. Any of the above

36. If a spark plug was fouled, what would happen to the HC emissions from the tail pipe?

    a. Increase
    b. Decrease
    c. No change
    d. Stay the same until about 2500 rpm, and then increase

37. Mechanic A says that a kinked vacuum sensing hose going to the gulp valve can cause a lean mixture on deceleration.

    Mechanic B says that engine backfire on deceleration can result if the sensing hose is kinked.

    Who is right?

    a. Mechanic A
    b. Mechanic B
    c. Both A and B
    d. Neither A nor B

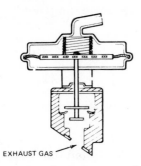

EXHAUST GAS

38. Mechanic A says that the valve pictured above should reduce $NO_x$ emissions if it is operating properly.

Mechanic B says that the valve pictured above should not be open at engine idle.

Who is right?

a. Mechanic A
b. Mechanic B
c. Both A and B
d. Neither A nor B

39. When is the ballast resistor not in operation in the coil primary circuit?

Mechanic A says when the engine starting system is used.

Mechanic B says when the engine is running at high speed.

Who is right?

a. Mechanic A
b. Mechanic B
c. Both A and B
d. Neither A nor B

40. Mechanic A says that a typical TCS system would deny distributor vacuum advance until about 35 mph.

Mechanic B says that most TCS systems use an exhaust gas recirculation valve for diluting the intake mixture.

Who is right?

a. Mechanic A
b. Mechanic B
c. Both A and B
d. Neither A nor B

41. Two mechanics are having a discussion about spark plugs.

    Mechanic A says that the spark plug gap setting on vehicles with
    electronic ignition may be as high as .080 inch.

    Mechanic B says that a resistor spark plug increases the voltage
    required to jump the gap by about 40%.

    Who is right?

    a. Mechanic A
    b. Mechanic B
    c. Both A and B
    d. Neither A nor B

42. Which statement below is true?

    a. A spark plug that does not use a gasket should be tightened
       less than one that uses a gasket.
    b. If an engine is burning a little oil, you may get anti-fouling
       protection by installing auxiliary gap spark plugs.
    c. A normal plug's firing end will generally turn gray or tan in use.
    d. All of the above

43. Where is the fuel discharge hole for the carburetor idle circuit
    located?

    a. Slightly above the closed position of the throttle plate
    b. Slightly below the closed position of the throttle plate
    c. At the main discharge nozzle opening
    d. In the venturi cluster

44. What device is used in passenger car ignition systems to open and
    close the primary circuit?

    a. Transistor
    b. Breaker points
    c. Ignition switch
    d. All of the above

45. The above breaker point misalignment condition is corrected by:


   a. Bending the point pivot post
   b. Replacing the breaker plate
   c. Bending the stationary point bracket
   d. Bending the movable point arm


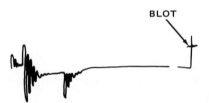

46. Refer to the superimposed oscilloscope pattern above.

   Mechanic A says that the "blot" indicates arcing points.

   Mechanic B says that the "blot" could be caused by a defective or
   incorrect capacity condenser.

   Who is right?


   a. Mechanic A
   b. Mechanic B
   c. Both A and B
   d. Neither A nor B

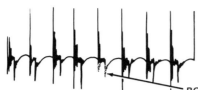

BOTTOM OF OSCILLATION LOST INTERMITTENTLY

47. The bottom of the parade pattern oscillation is lost intermittently (see above). Why?

   Mechanic A says that spark plug wires could be routed incorrectly causing a cross-fire.

   Mechanic B says that the cap could be cracked.

   Who is right?

   a. Mechanic A
   b. Mechanic B
   c. Both A and B
   d. Neither A nor B

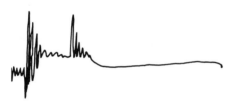

48. A customer has a hard start complaint. You observe the above secondary superimposed pattern. What is wrong?

   a. The coil is shorted.
   b. The condenser has series resistance.
   c. The coil is hooked up backwards.
   d. The rotor air gap is excessive.

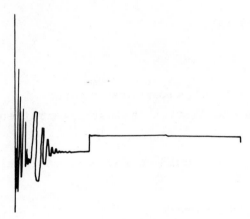

49. The scope pattern shown above is a:


    a. Raster pattern
    b. Primary pattern
    c. Secondary parade pattern
    d. Solid state ignition system secondary pattern

50. What are the large oscillations directly to the right of the spark
    plug firing line (see above)?


    a. Coil build-up (saturation) time
    b. Dwell time
    c. Plug wire resistance peaks
    d. Coil and condenser discharge action


51. You are going to perform a capacity test on a 12-volt battery.  What
    is the proper load to apply?


    a. 2 times the ampere-hour rating for 5 seconds
    b. 3 times the ampere-hour rating for 15 seconds
    c. 4 times the ampere-hour rating for 30 seconds
    d. 150 amps for 45 seconds

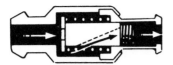

52. In the device above, the plunger is stuck in the maximum flow
    position.

    Mechanic A says that this will cause a rough engine idle.

    Mechanic B says that this will cause excessive oil consumption.

    Who is right?


    a. Mechanic A
    b. Mechanic B
    c. Both A and B
    d. Neither A nor B


**FRONT OF ENGINE**

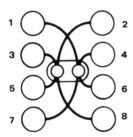

53. Refer to the above intake manifold design.  When doing a minor tune-
    up the mechanic observes that spark plugs 5, 6, 7, and 8 are
    blistered.  The rest of the plugs are O.K.  What could be the problem?


    a. A lean mixture at the right-hand carburetor barrel
    b. A clogged or restricted cooling system
    c. Either a or b
    d. Neither a nor b

54. A mechanic is performing a compression test on an engine.  Which statement below is correct?

    a. All cylinders reading higher than normal could be caused by excessive carbon accumulation.
    b. All cylinders reading even, but considerably lower than normal, could be caused by a slipped timing chain.
    c. Low identical readings on two adjacent cylinders could be caused by a blown head gasket.
    d. All of the above

55. A cylinder leakage test is being performed.  When air is introduced into the cylinder, bubbles are seen in the radiator at the filler opening.  What does this possibly indicate?

    a. A cracked cylinder block
    b. A blown head gasket
    c. Either a or b
    d. Neither a nor b

56. Mechanic A says that breaker point spring tension is read when the rubbing block is on the distributor cam high point.

    Mechanic B says that spring tension is read when the contact points just separate.

    Who is right?

    a. Mechanic A
    b. Mechanic B
    c. Both A and B
    d. Neither A nor B

57. Point pitting (metal transfer between contacts) can be caused by:

    a. Incorrect condenser capacity
    b. Prolonged idling periods
    c. A missing ground strap between the back of the engine and the firewall
    d. All of the above

58. You are testing a distributor on a testing machine. Eight strobo-scope images appear. You compare the positions of the stroboscope images as they index the degree scale. The images vary plus or minus 4 degrees from the normal 45 degree spacing interval. What does this indicate?

    a. A worn upper distributor shaft bushing
    b. A dirty advance weight mechanism
    c. Both a and b
    d. Neither a nor b

**GLOWING CARBON PARTICLE**

59. The picture above illustrates what combustion chamber situation?

    a. Detonation
    b. Over-advanced timing
    c. Pre-ignition
    d. Normal burning

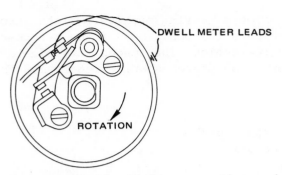

60. You are static timing an engine using a dwell meter as a continuity tester (see above drawing). The ignition switch is in the off position.

    Mechanic A says to rotate the distributor body against rotation until the meter shows no current flow, then slowly rotate the body with rotation until the meter just indicates full current flow.

    Mechanic B says to rotate the distributor body in the direction of rotation until the meter shows that the points have just opened.

    Who is right?


    a. Mechanic A
    b. Mechanic B
    c. Both A and B
    d. Neither A nor B


61. You suspect that an exhaust pipe has collapsed on the inside. A vacuum gauge is hooked up to the intake manifold. What might the gauge read if a restriction is present?


    a. At idle there is a regular needle drop of about 3 to 8 inches.
    b. At idle there is a regular needle drop of about 8 inches.
    c. At 1000 engine rpm the needle shows a continuous gradual drop.
    d. At idle the needle oscillates slowly between 16-21 inches.

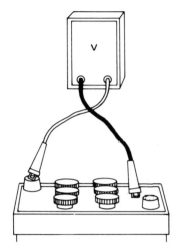

62. What is the mechanic checking for in the picture above?


    a. Cable corrosion
    b. Cell voltage
    c. Battery leakage
    d. None of the above


63. A 12-volt battery removed from a vehicle has been sitting on a shelf for 4 months.  How should this battery be put back into service?


    a. Dump the old electrolyte, fill with new electrolyte, and recharge.
    b. Put on half the normal charging rate for 50 to 100 hours.
    c. Either a or b
    d. Neither a nor b


64. A cranking vacuum test reading is lower than specification.  This could result in:


    a. Hard starting
    b. Rough idle
    c. Both a and b
    d. Neither a nor b

65. Mechanic A says that an intake manifold gasket leak can cause spark plug fouling.

   Mechanic B says that an intake manifold gasket leak can cause oil consumption.

   Who is right?

   a. Mechanic A
   b. Mechanic B
   c. Both A and B
   d. Neither A nor B

66. A customer complains that the engine keeps running after the key is turned off.

   Mechanic A says that carbon deposits in the combustion chambers could be the cause.

   Mechanic B says that the idle speed could be set too high or the solenoid throttle stop plunger is stuck.

   Who is right?

   a. Mechanic A
   b. Mechanic B
   c. Both A and B
   d. Neither A nor B

67. A V-8 engine is operating at 70 mph (3000 rpm). How many times will the breaker points open and close in a minute?

   a. 4,800
   b. 12,000
   c. 18,000
   d. 24,000

68. Dwell on the distributor pictured above:


    a. Can be set with the engine idling
    b. Is set by raising the window and inserting an allen wrench
    c. Both a and b
    d. Neither a nor b

69. The carburetor part shown above is designed to allow for:


    a. Easier cold starting
    b. Easier hot starting
    c. The prevention of "dieseling"
    d. A richer mixture during hot weather


70. You are rebuilding a carburetor.  Which of the following can be
    ruined by soaking in carburetor cleaner?


    a. Choke pull-off (vacuum break)
    b. Hot idle compensating valve
    c. Throttle positioner diaphragm
    d. All of the above

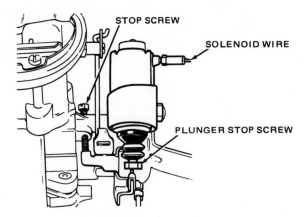

71. Many carburetors are equipped with an idle stop solenoid (see above).

Mechanic A says that hot engine idle speed is adjusted by turning the plunger stop screw with the solenoid wire connected.

Mechanic B says that low speed idle is adjusted by turning the stop screw with the solenoid wire disconnected.

Who is right?


a. Mechanic A
b. Mechanic B
c. Both A and B
d. Neither A nor B

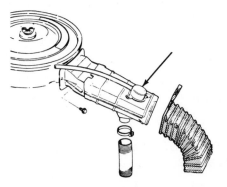

72. What is the name of the part that the arrow above is pointing to?


a. Air bleed valve
b. Thermostat
c. Vacuum motor
d. Temperature sensor

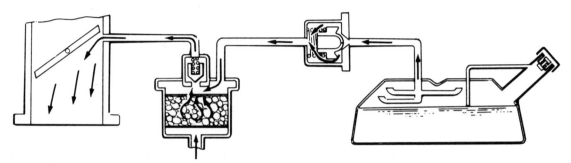

73. Refer to the evaporative control system illustrated above.  What is passing into the intake manifold?


    a. Liquid gas
    b. Evaporated gas
    c. Fresh air
    d. Both b and c


74. How is intake manifold vacuum related to engine load?

    Mechanic A says that intake manifold vacuum and engine load are not related.

    Mechanic B says that the more the load, the more the vacuum.

    Who is right?


    a. Mechanic A
    b. Mechanic B
    c. Both A and B
    d. Neither A nor B


75. High voltage is produced in the ignition coil secondary winding when:


    a. The condenser shorts out.
    b. The points close.
    c. The points open.
    d. The rotor makes contact.

76. A "hot" spark plug:

    a. Has a long heat travel path
    b. Has a short heat travel path
    c. Is advisable for continuous high speed driving
    d. Produces less radio interference

77. Mechanic A says that the centrifugal spark advance mechanism adjusts ignition timing to suit changes in load.

    Mechanic B says that it adjusts ignition timing to suit changes in speed.

    Who is right?

    a. Mechanic A
    b. Mechanic B
    c. Both A and B
    d. Neither A nor B

78. Rapid burning of ignition breaker points may be caused by:

    a. Improper voltage regulator adjustment
    b. Incorrect point gap
    c. Both a and b
    d. Neither a nor b

79. Many cars use a device to prevent engine stalling due to automatic transmission drag when they stop suddenly. What is the name of this item?

    a. A dashpot
    b. A kickdown lever
    c. An elastomer valve
    d. An over-travel spring

80. Under what condition would carburetor "icing" most likely occur?

    a. Low humidity
    b. High humidity
    c. When water is in the gasoline
    d. At any temperature below freezing

81. Some carburetors are designed with a choke lock-out.

   Mechanic A says that the purpose of the lock-out is to prevent the choke from closing once the engine is warm.

   Mechanic B says that the lock-out prevents the secondaries from opening when the choke is closed.

   Who is right?

   a. Mechanic A
   b. Mechanic B
   c. Both A and B
   d. Neither A nor B

82. Which of the following statements is true?

   a. Using leaded fuel can poison and neutralize the effectiveness of a catalytic converter.
   b. An open spark plug wire can increase the temperature in the catalytic converter to as much as 1800°F.
   c. Contaminated pellets in General Motors catalytic converters can be replaced.
   d. All of the above

83. What would cause a high spark plug firing voltage?

   a. Excessive resistance in the plug wires
   b. Wide plug gap
   c. Either a or b
   d. Neither a nor b

84. In a Chevrolet V-8 engine, the No. 1 piston is at TDC on compression. What position is No. 6 piston in?

   a. Half the distance up on compression
   b. Half the distance down on power
   c. TDC
   d. BDC

85. An engine is running in the shop at fast idle.  With a normally
    operating carburetor, when the air horn is partly covered with a
    piece of cardboard, the engine should:

    a. Slow down
    b. Speed up
    c. Surge
    d. Quit running

86. A cylinder has a very low compression reading.  When 40 wt. oil is
    squirted into the spark plug hole, the compression increases to a
    normal reading.  What engine defect is indicated?

    a. A bad valve
    b. Defective piston rings
    c. A casting crack in the cylinder head
    d. A broken head gasket divider

87. In a closed crankcase system, the blow-by gases are routed through
    the:

    a. Intake manifold
    b. Air cleaner
    c. Both a and b
    c. Neither a nor b

88. A vacuum advance unit that uses "ported spark" receives its vacuum
    from the carburetor:

    a. Venturi
    b. Air horn
    c. Just below the throttle plates
    d. Just above the throttle plates

89. What component is not in the primary ignition circuit?

    a. Points
    b. Condenser
    c. Rotor
    d. Key switch

90. Mechanic A says that the centrifugal advance mechanism rotates the cam in the same direction as distributor rotation.

   Mechanic B says that the centrifugal advance mechanism varies spark timing according to engine speed.

   Who is right?

   a. Mechanic A
   b. Mechanic B
   c. Both A and B
   d. Neither A nor B

91. One voltmeter prod is grounded on the radiator. The other prod is inserted into the coolant. A reading of 4 volts is obtained. What does this indicate?

   a. Drain, flush, and refill the cooling system.
   b. Corrosion is taking place.
   c. Both a and b
   d. Neither a nor b

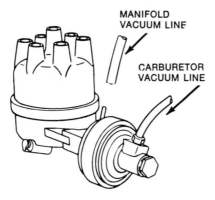

MANIFOLD VACUUM LINE

CARBURETOR VACUUM LINE

92. An engine is operating at idle speed. The carburetor vacuum line is connected to the outer diaphragm (see picture above). When the manifold vacuum line is connected to the inner diaphragm, what should happen to spark timing?

   a. It should advance.
   b. It should retard.
   c. It will change and speed up the engine.
   d. Nothing will happen at this speed.

93. What is the air injection system component pictured above?

    a. Air pump relief valve
    b. Check valve
    c. Diverter valve
    d. Dump valve

94. You are using a battery post adapter switch when testing an alternator system.  What position should the switch be in when reading alternator output?

    a. Open
    b. Closed
    c. Half-way open
    d. In the grounded position

95. Mechanic A says that in a car with a negative grounded battery, the distributor primary lead should be connected to the positive terminal on the coil.

    Mechanic B says that when a DC voltmeter is connected with the positive prod attached to the engine ground and the negative prod momentarily touched to the spark plug terminal (engine running), the needle should swing upscale if coil polarity is correct.

    Who is right?

    a. Mechanic A
    b. Mechanic B
    c. Both A and B
    d. Neither A nor B

96. The infrared exhaust emission analyzer is being discussed by two mechanics.

Mechanic A says that a high HC reading at idle indicates an ignition, vacuum, or valve malfunction.

Mechanic B says that a high CO reading at idle could be caused by a leaky or stuck power valve.

Who is right?

a. Mechanic A
b. Mechanic B
c. Both A and B
d. Neither A nor B

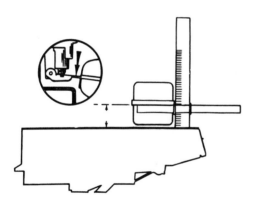

97. What adjustment procedure is shown above?

a. Float level
b. Float drop
c. Float alignment
d. Checking clearance between the float toe and the fuel reservoir wall

98. When setting basic ignition timing, which of the following statements is true?

    a. The distributor vacuum lines are generally disconnected and plugged.
    b. To advance the timing, rotate the distributor in the direction of rotor rotation.
    c. Both a and b
    d. Neither a nor b

99. A car owner complains of erratic performance.  A mechanic checks the timing.  He notices that the timing marks don't return to the same spot when the rpms are raised, then dropped.  What could be causing this problem?

    a. The weight and cam assembly needs lubrication
    b. A worn breaker plate
    c. Both a and b
    d. Neither a nor b

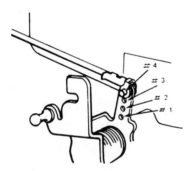

100. On the carburetor shown in the picture above, what would happen if the rod was moved to hole #1?

    a. The accelerating pump stroke will be changed.
    b. The curb idle speed will change.
    c. The fast idle cam position will change.
    d. None  of the above will change.

101. A car is originally equipped with a vented gas tank cap. What can happen if someone puts a nonvented cap on the tank?

Mechanic A says that gas tank will collapse.

Mechanic B says that the car will be starved for fuel, especially at high speeds.

Who is right?

a. Mechanic A
b. Mechanic B
c. Both A and B
d. Neither A nor B

102. The manifold heat control valve (heat riser) should be serviced when performing a tune-up using which of the following procedures?

a. Lubricate the valve with 30 wt. engine oil.
b. Disassemble the valve, clean, and reassemble.
c. Apply recommended lubricant to shaft ends; tap the valve lightly if necessary for free action.
d. Install a new valve.

103. What will happen when the infrared analyzer probe is placed near a fuel line leak?

Mechanic A says that only a CO reading will be obtained.

Mechanic B says that both an HC and CO reading will be obtained.

Who is right?

a. Mechanic A
b. Mechanic B
c. Both A and B
d. Neither A nor B

104. Two mechanics are discussing infrared analyzer meter readings.

   Mechanic A says that an engine vacuum leak will cause the CO reading to be higher than normal.

   Mechanic B says that an engine misfire will have little or no effect on the CO reading.

   Who is right?

   a. Mechanic A
   b. Mechanic B
   c. Both A and B
   d. Neither A nor B

105. On a four stroke cycle V-8 engine, how much does the crankshaft turn between each spark?

   a. 1/4 turn
   b. 1/2 turn
   c. 1/8 turn
   d. 3/4 turn

106. How is the ignition system condenser connected in relation to the points?

   a. Series parallel
   b. Series
   c. Parallel
   d. Grounded to the primary side

107. The primary ignition circuit on a vehicle is good.  There is no spark coming out of the coil high tension wire.  This could be caused by:

   a. A defective coil
   b. Closed contact points
   c. A grounded rotor
   d. All of the above

108. A good spark is coming out of the coil high tension wire, but the engine will not start.  Which of the following could be the reason?

    a. An open condenser
    b. A carbon tracked distributor cap
    c. A broken primary pigtail lead
    d. All of the above

109. A mechanic performs a minor tune-up on a car.  After 50 miles of driving, the car owner complains of rough idle and misfire.  A check shows the dwell to be way out of specification.  What could have caused this to happen?

    a. A defective condenser
    b. No cam lubricant was used.
    c. The point hold-down screw was not tightened correctly.
    d. All of the above

110. In what carburetor circuit might a discharge weight be found?

    a. Float circuit
    b. High speed circuit
    c. Pump circuit
    d. Power circuit

111. What would be correct procedure when replacing a relief valve on an air pump?

    a. Remove the valve by twisting back and forth with a pipe wrench.
    b. Have the pump disassembled, and install the valve by using a large hammer and a piece of pipe for a driver.
    c. Both a and b
    d. Neither a nor b

# 5
# AUTOMATIC TRANSMISSIONS

STUDY OUTLINE

I.  Basic Gear Systems

    A. Speed vs. Torque
    B. Gear Ratios


II.  Planetary Gear Systems

    A. Construction
    B. Principles of Operation

        1. Rules of planetary gears
        2. Typical transmission power flow
        3. How various ratios can be obtained

            a. Hold one member
            b. Drive two members
            c. Neutral

        4. Compound Planetary

            a. Used in pairs or as a multiple unit


III.  Friction Elements

    A. Basic Principles of Hydraulics
    B. Hydraulic System Components (Identification of Parts and Operation)

        1. Reservoir (sump)
        2. Pump
        3. Valving

            a. Pressure regulator
            b. Manual valve
            c. Governor valve
            d. Shift valve
            e. Throttle modulator valve

C. Torque Converters

    1. Elements of the converter
    2. Principles of converter operation
    3. Stator operation

D. Fluids

    1. General Motors (Dexron)
    2. Ford

E. Bands, Clutches, One-way Clutches
F. Servos

IV. Transmission, Light Duty Service

A. Oil Level and Condition (Draining and Refilling)
B. Linkage Adjustments

    1. Manual
    2. Throttle
    3. Neutral start systems

C. Vacuum Modulators ("Weighing" and Adjustment)
D. Leaks (Seal and Gasket Replacement)
E. Filters
F. Band Adjustment

V. Transmission Overhaul Procedures

A. Required End-play and Clearance Checks
B. Inspection of Components

    1. Foreign material in pan
    2. Gears
    3. Pumps
    4. Bands and clutches
    5. Machined surfaces
    6. Control valves
    7. Converter assembly
    8. Turbine shaft
    9. Flex plate

C. Seals

1. Metal clad
2. Lip
3. Flat and o-ring
4. Metal seal rings
5. Plastic

D. Bushings

1. Installation tools

E. Thrust Washers

1. Torrington
2. Plastic
3. Phenolic resin

F. Assembly of Components (Be Familiar With the Following Procedures)

1. Clutch soak
2. Converter flush
3. Install valve body following torque specifications
4. Indexing the manual shift valve
5. Indexing the throttle valve
6. Pump clearance checks
7. Lubing the converter hub
8. Converter drive lug installation position
9. Flushing cooler lines
10. Checking stator end-play
11. Speedometer gear installation

VI. Problem/Diagnosis

A. No Drive
B. Drive in One Range Only
C. Moves in Range Other Than One Selected

1. Motor mounts
2. Bent linkage
3. Linkage adjustment
4. Transmission mount

D. Noises/Problems

1. Pumps
2. Friction plates
3. Bands
4. Gears

E. Vacuum Modulators

   1. Late shift
   2. Early shift
   3. Rough downshift
   4. Rough upshift
   5. Checking vacuum
   6. Exhaust smoke

F. Shifting, Late and Early
G. Rough Shifting (Up and Down)
H. Vehicle Does not Hold in "P"
I. Slip on Upshifts
J. Harsh Engagement in Any Gear
K. No Downshift
L. Leaks

   1. External
   2. Internal

M. Converter

   1. Stall testing procedures
   2. Slipping one-way clutch
   3. Frozen stator

N. Tests

   1. Pressure (test plug location)
   2. Vacuum
   3. Air

---

EXERCISES

1. Mechanic A says that "Dexron" ATF was developed by Ford engineers as an improvement over "Type A, Suffix A" fluid.

   Mechanic B says that "Dexron" ATF is designed for transmissions having low friction, soft shift qualities.

   Who is right?

   a. Mechanic A
   b. Mechanic B
   c. Both A and B
   d. Neither A nor B

2. "Type F" transmission fluid:

   a. Is a high friction type oil
   b. Is a firm shift oil
   c. Both a and b
   d. Neither a nor b

3. Which one of the following is not a part of the fluid coupling?

   a. Pump
   b. Driven member
   c. Stator
   d. Turbine

4. What component of the torque converter is attached to the transmission input shaft?

   a. Pump
   b. Impeller
   c. Turbine
   d. Stator

5. Mechanic A says that torque is multiplied in a torque converter because the stator blades redirect fluid back to the impeller.

   Mechanic B says that the stator is used when starting the vehicle from a standstill.

   Who is right?

   a. Mechanic A
   b. Mechanic B
   c. Both A and B
   d. Neither A nor B

6. During conditions of high vortex:

   a. The one-way clutch is locked up.
   b. The one-way clutch is unlocked.
   c. Fluid is redirected to the turbine.
   d. None of the above.

7. If any two members of a planetary gear set are locked, what would the ratio be?

   a. 3 to 1
   b. 2 to 1
   c. 2 to 3
   d. None of the above

8. The sun gear is being held in a simple planetary gear set. The ring gear is the driver, and the carrier is driven. What would be the result?

   a. Forward gear reduction
   b. Forward speed increase
   c. Reverse gear
   d. Direct drive

9. Which of the following is a planetary gearbox holding device?

   a. Multiple disc clutch
   b. Double or single wrapped band and servo
   c. One-way clutch
   d. All of the above

10. Mechanic A says that the above automatic transmission component is a sprag clutch.

    Mechanic B says that it is a one-way clutch.

    Who is right?

    a. Mechanic A
    b. Mechanic B
    c. Both A and B
    d. Neither A nor B

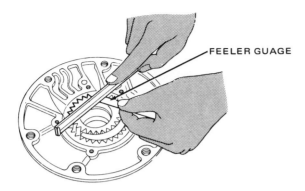

FEELER GUAGE

11. The picture above shows a mechanic checking a front pump for:

    a. Cover warpage
    b. Crescent tip clearance
    c. Body face to drive gear face clearance
    d. Body face to driven gear face clearance

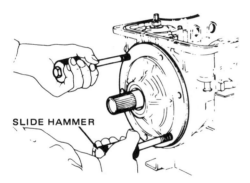

SLIDE HAMMER

12. What is being done in the picture above?

    a. Aligning the stator support
    b. Installing the planetary carrier
    c. Removing the governor body support
    d. Removing the front oil pump

13. An engine starts with the automatic transmission gear selector in
    any position. What is the most likely reason?

    a. A shorted neutral safety switch
    b. An open neutral safety switch
    c. A grounded transmission regulated spark switch
    d. A shorted ignition switch

14. A car owner says that his automatic transmission is not shifting right.  During a road test the mechanic finds all upshifts are very late under light throttle pressure.  What could be the problem?

    a. Excessive modulator pressure
    b. A faulty governor
    c. Either a or b
    d. Neither a nor b

15. Stall test rpm is below specifications in D, 2, and 1 driving ranges.

    Mechanic A says that the one-way clutch in the converter could be slipping.

    Mechanic B says that the engine could be in need of a tune-up.

    Who is right?

    a. Mechanic A
    b. Mechanic B
    c. Both A and B
    d. Neither A nor B

16. Mechanic A says that gummy varnish deposits on the transmission dipstick indicate prolonged fluid overheating.

    Mechanic B says that anti-freeze has found its way into the transmission.

    Who is right?

    a. Mechanic A
    b. Mechanic B
    c. Either A or B
    d. Neither A nor B

17. Mechanic A says that overfilling an automatic transmission can result in slipping.

   Mechanic B says that overfilling can cause fluid aeration.

   Who is right?

   a. Mechanic A
   b. Mechanic B
   c. Both A and B
   d. Neither A nor B

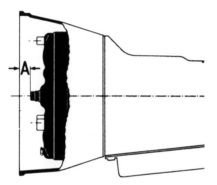

18. Mechanic A says that the correct measurement above will insure that the converter hub is fully engaged in the pump gear.

   Mechanic B says that the dimension above is a converter end-play measurement.

   Who is right?

   a. Mechanic A
   b. Mechanic B
   c. Both A and B
   d. Neither A nor B

19. A very common cause of "stop sign creeping" in a car equipped with an automatic transmission is:

    a. The ATF level is too high.
    b. A defective governor
    c. Multiple clutch disc wear
    d. An incorrect idle speed adjustment

20. When does the stator overrunning clutch unlock?

    a. Under acceleration
    b. During stall
    c. In passing gear
    d. At coupling speed

21. Mechanic A says that the throttle valve in automatic transmissions is activated by mechanical linkage.

    Mechanic B says that the throttle valve is activated by a vacuum diaphragm.

    Who is right?

    a. Mechanic A
    b. Mechanic B
    c. Either A or B
    d. Neither A nor B

22. Mechanic A says that a stall test is performed on an automatic transmission to determine if the converter sprag assembly is slipping.

    Mechanic B says that a stall test is performed to determine if the bands and clutches are holding.

    Who is right?

    a. Mechanic A
    b. Mechanic B
    c. Both A and B
    d. Neither A nor B

23. Mechanic A says that "sagging" engine mounts can alter the TV rod adjustment.

   Mechanic B says that "sagging" engine mounts can alter the downshift cable adjustment.

   Who is right?

   a. Mechanic A
   b. Mechanic B
   c. Both A and B
   d. Neither A nor B

24. Mechanic A says that a vacuum modulator is used on automatic transmissions to regulate pressure to the governor.

   Mechanic B says that a vacuum modulator is used to sense any change in the torque input to the transmission.

   Who is right?

   a. Mechanic A
   b. Mechanic B
   c. Both A and B
   d. Neither A nor B

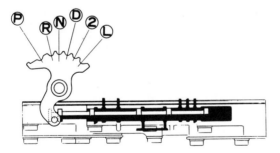

25. The spool valve pictured above is a:

   a. Pressure regulator valve
   b. Sequence valve
   c. Accumulator valve
   d. Manual valve

26. Mechanic A says that automatic transmission shift valves are
    operated by governor pressure.

    Mechanic B says that shift valves are operated by main control
    pressure.

    Who is right?


    a. Mechanic A
    b. Mechanic B
    c. Both A and B
    d. Neither A nor B


27. Mechanic A says that automatic transmission multiple disc clutches
    are generally engaged by spring pressure and disengaged by a
    hydraulic piston.

    Mechanic B says that multiple disc clutches can be used only to hold a drum.

    Who is right?


    a. Mechanic A
    b. Mechanic B
    c. Both A and B
    d. Neither A nor B


28. An automatic transmission shift valve:


    a. Is a pressure regulating valve
    b. Must be manually preset
    c. Is a diaphragm type valve
    d. Is a control valve operated by oil pressure

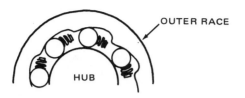

29. The above illustration shows an overrunning clutch.

    Mechanic A says that if the hub is held, the outer race can turn clockwise.

    Mechanic B says that if the outer race is held, the hub can turn counter-clockwise.

    Who is right?


    a. Mechanic A
    b. Mechanic B
    c. Both A and B
    d. Neither A nor B

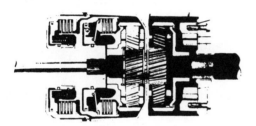

30. Refer to the two planetary gear transmission above.  How is high gear obtained?

    Mechanic A says by applying the front clutch and the rear band.

    Mechanic B says by locking the sun and ring gears together.

    Who is right?


    a. Mechanic A
    b. Mechanic B
    c. Both A and B
    d. Neither A nor B

31. A low automatic transmission oil pressure reading could be caused by:

    a. A stuck pressure regulating valve
    b. A worn pump
    c. Low fluid level
    d. All of the above

32. If the pressure regulator valve spring tension were increased:

    a. The system pressure would decrease.
    b. More pump pressure would be required to move the valve into
       the bleed-off position.
    c. Both a and b
    d. Neither a nor b

33. If an automatic transmission vehicle does not have a rear pump:

    a. It cannot be push-started.
    b. Oil will not be circulated through the transmission unless the
       engine is running.
    c. Both a and b
    d. Neither a nor b

34. Mechanic A says that engine speed should change when the hose is
    pulled off the vacuum modulator.

    Mechanic B says that a slight amount of transmission fluid should be
    present in the vacuum side of the modulator.

    Who is right?

    a. Mechanic A
    b. Mechanic B
    c. Both A and B
    d. Neither A nor B

35. Which of the following statements is true?

    a. Automatic transmissions must be in "D" range for an accurate fluid level check.
    b. The dipstick "add" mark indicates that the fluid level is generally one quart low.
    c. Most late model automatic transmissions do not have a fluid drain plug in the pan.
    d. All of the above

Cape Chisel

36. What is the mechanic removing in the picture above?

    a. The stator support bushing
    b. The high clutch hub bushing
    c. The center support sleeve
    d. The sun gear input shell

37. Mechanic A says that as a vehicle gets older the engine vacuum drops and a lower modulator pressure results.

    Mechanic B says that the higher the engine vacuum, the higher the modulator pressure.

    Who is right?

    a. Mechanic A
    b. Mechanic B
    c. Both A and B
    d. Neither A nor B

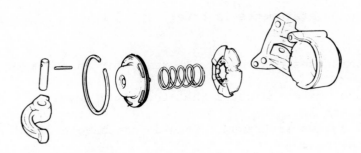

38. The automatic transmission part shown above:

    a. Is hydraulically actuated
    b. Actuates a band
    c. Both a and b
    d. Neither a nor b

39. Mechanic A says that the automatic transmission front pump operates
    when the engine is cranking.

    Mechanic B says that the front pump is driven by drive lugs (dogs)
    on the end of the torque converter housing.

    Who is right?

    a. Mechanic A
    b. Mechanic B
    c. Both A and B
    d. Neither A nor B

40. The governor valve:

    a. Is located on the output shaft
    b. Senses road speed
    c. Nearly closes off the exhaust as vehicle speed increases
    d. All of the above

41. A vehicle has a slight flare between upshifts.  What would be the first thing to check?

    a. Governor
    b. Valve body
    c. Intermediate servo
    d. Fluid level

42. You are servicing a valve body.

Mechanic A says that a magnet can be used to remove any sticking valves.

Mechanic B says that a plastic stick should be used to poke out sticking valves.

Who is right?

    a. Mechanic A
    b. Mechanic B
    c. Either a or B
    d. Neither A nor B

43. You are installing an automatic transmission.  What type of lubricant should you apply to the pilot hole in the drive plate (see above)?

    a. Petroleum jelly
    b. ATF
    c. Wheel bearing grease
    d. No lubricant is necessary.

44. The automatic transmission fluid in a vehicle is foamy and milky appearing.

    Mechanic A says that rain water may have entered because the dipstick was not pushed down all the way.

    Mechanic B says that a broken heat exchanger in the radiator may be the problem.

    Who is right?

    a. Mechanic A
    b. Mechanic B
    c. Either A or B
    d. Neither A nor B

45. When new composition clutch plates are used, Mechanic A says to soak the plates in ATF for 15 minutes before they are assembled.

    Mechanic B says to coat the friction plate surfaces with vaseline prior to installation.

    Who is right?

    a. Mechanic A
    b. Mechanic B
    c. Either A or B
    d. Neither A nor B

46. Clutch pack apply pistons are returned by:

    a. A Belleville spring
    b. A series of small coil springs
    c. A large coil spring
    d. All of the above

47. Mechanic A says that a double wrap band has better holding ability than a single wrap band.

    Mechanic B says that a double wrap band requires more servo force to create the same holding effort as a single wrap band.

    Who is right?

    a. Mechanic A
    b. Mechanic B
    c. Both A and B
    d. Neither A nor B

48. When an automatic transmission is in high gear (direct drive), the power flow is generally through:

    a. Multiple disc clutches
    b. One-way clutches
    c. Bands
    d. Servos

49. Mechanic A says that band adjustment is made to be sure the band does not drag on the drum in the release position.

    Mechanic B says that band adjustment is made to keep the servo from bottoming as it is applied.

    Who is right?

    a. Mechanic A
    b. Mechanic B
    c. Both A and B
    d. Neither A nor B

50. A vehicle is making a forced downshift for acceleration. Which of the following is true?

    a. The detent valve controls the shift.
    b. The governor pressure is overcome.
    c. Both a and b
    d. Neither a nor b

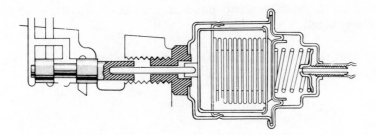

51. What statement is true with reference to the picture above?


    a. The diaphragm is altitude compensated.
    b. Control pressure is increased by turning the adjusting screw
       counter-clockwise.
    c. Both a and b
    d. Neither a nor b

**SCALE**

52. The mechanic above is:


    a. Checking for ruptured bellows
    b. Checking the modulator setting by "weighing"
    c. Both a and b
    d. Neither a nor b

53. The picture above shows:

    a. Installing the rear pump seal
    b. Installing the extension housing seal
    c. Installing the rear bushing
    d. None of the above

54. Slight burrs and nicks can be removed from valve body valves by using:

    a. A file
    b. Emery paper
    c. Crocus cloth
    d. A wire wheel

55. Mechanic A says that a chipped planetary gear tooth would cause transmission noise in any forward gear.

Mechanic B says that a damaged speedometer drive gear would cause noise in all drive gears.

Who is right?

    a. Mechanic A
    b. Mechanic B
    c. Both A and B
    d. Neither A nor B

56. A vehicle has "no engine braking in manual second gear." What could be the cause of this problem?

    a. Linkage
    b. Band adjustment
    c. Either a or b
    d. Neither a nor b

57. Mechanic A says that accelerator (throttle) linkage should be adjusted before the kickdown or downshift linkage is set.

    Mechanic B says that accelerator (throttle) linkage should be adjusted before manual (shift) linkage is set.

    Who is right?

    a. Mechanic A
    b. Mechanic B
    c. Both A and B
    d. Neither A nor B

58. An automatic transmission shifts directly from 1 to 3 in drive range. What could be the cause of this problem?

    a. The intermediate band adjustment
    b. The governor
    c. Either a or b
    d. Neither a nor b

59. Endwise (thrust) movement of automatic transmission shafts and drums is controlled by:

    a. Torrington needle bearings
    b. Phenolic resin thrust washers
    c. Nylon thrust washers
    d. All of the above

60. Mechanic A says that clutch pack plates are stacked alternately when assembled (steel, lined, steel, etc.).

    Mechanic B says that plates are generally dished when new.

    Who is right?

    a. Mechanic A
    b. Mechanic B
    c. Both A and B
    d. Neither A nor B

61. Internal leakage in the automatic transmission is controlled by:


    a. Cast iron seals
    b. O-ring seals
    c. Lip type seals
    d. All of the above

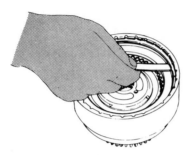

62. The mechanic in the picture above is:


    a. Measuring snap ring to plate clearance
    b. Installing the multiple disc square-cut seal
    c. Removing the clutch drum retaining plate
    d. None of the above

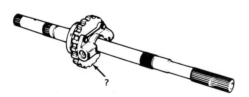

63. The arrow in the picture above is pointing to:


    a. The parking gear
    b. The low-reverse clutch hub
    c. The governor valve
    d. The stator support

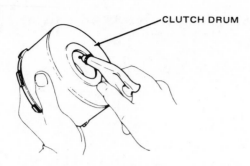

CLUTCH DRUM

64. What is being done in the picture above?

    a. Popping out the sun gear snap ring
    b. Blowing out the clutch piston
    c. Removing stuck one-way clutch rollers
    d. None of the above

65. A vehicle does not move in any gear range.

    Mechanic A says that clutch and band material that has clogged the
    oil screen could be the reason.

    Mechanic B says that oil pump internal leakage could be the reason.

    Who is right?

    a. Mechanic A
    b. Mechanic B
    c. Both A and B
    d. Neither A nor B

66. If the converter pump drive hub is lightly scored:

    a. Install a new converter.
    b. Polish the hub with 600 grit crocus cloth.
    c. Have the hub turned down on a lathe.
    d. Dress the scored surface with a mill smooth file.

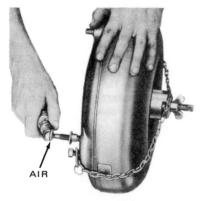

67. The picture above shows:


    a. A converter being flushed
    b. A converter leakage test
    c. The stator clutch being tested for lock-up
    d. All of the above

68. What is the mechanic doing in the picture above?


    a. Pulling the secondary sun gear
    b. Pulling the rear pump drive
    c. Installing the reverse ring gear
    d. Removing the speedometer drive gear

69. The picture above shows the mechanic:

   a. Removing the front pump seal
   b. Removing the front pump
   c. Removing the pump housing bushing
   d. None of the above

70. A car owner complains of harsh, late shifts.  This could result from:

   a. A broken diaphragm in the vacuum modulator
   b. A lack of vacuum at the vacuum modulator
   c. Either a or b
   d. Neither a nor b

| Throttle | Range | Shift | 1 | 2 | 3 | 4 | 5 | 6 |
|---|---|---|---|---|---|---|---|---|
| Closed | D | 1-2 | 8-9 | 8-10 | 8-9 | 7-9 | 7-8 | 6-8 |
| (Above | D | 2-3 | 8-21 | 8-21 | 8-19 | 7-19 | 7-18 | 6-18 |
| 17" | D | 3-1 | 8-9 | 8-10 | 8-9 | 7-9 | 7-8 | 6-8 |
| Vacuum) | 1 | 2-1 | 26-34 | 25-33 | 24-32 | 23-31 | 22-29 | 21-29 |
| To Detent | D | 1-2 | 37-50 | 35-49 | 34-47 | 33-45 | 31-43 | 30-42 |
| (Torque | D | 2-3 | 64-82 | 61-79 | 59-76 | 57-74 | 55-70 | 52-68 |
| Demand) | D | 3-2 | 29-42 | 28-41 | 27-40 | 26-38 | 25-36 | 24-35 |
| Through | D | 1-2 | 49-57 | 47-55 | 43-53 | 44-51 | 42-49 | 40-47 |
| Detent | D | 2-3 | 84-93 | 80-90 | 78-87 | 75-84 | 72-80 | 69-78 |
| (W.O.T.) | D | 3-2 | 74-83 | 71-81 | 70-78 | 66-75 | 64-72 | 61-69 |
| | D | 3-1 or 2-1 | 37-43 | 35-42 | 34-40 | 33-39 | 31-37 | 30-35 |

| Axle Ratio | Tire Size | Use Column No. | Axle Ratio | Tire Size | Use Column No. |
|---|---|---|---|---|---|
| 2.80:1 | H78 x 15, 8.55 x 15 | 1 | 3.25:1 | H78 x 15, 8.55 x 15 | 5 |
| | H70 x 15 | | | H70 x 15 | |
| | 8.25 x 15, G78 x 15 | 2 | | 8.25 x 15, G78 x 15 | 6 |
| | 7.75 x 15, F78 x 15 | | | 7.75 x 15, F78 x 15 | |
| 3.00:1 | H78 x 15, 8.55 x 15 | 3 | | | |
| | H70 x 15 | | | | |
| | 8.25 x 15, G78 x 15 | 4 | | | |
| | 7.75 x 15, F78 x 15 | | | | |

71. Your car has a 3.00 to 1 axle ratio and is equipped with G78 x 15 tires. When pulling away from a stop sign under light throttle, at what speed should the 1 - 2 shift occur? Refer to the chart above.


a. 6 - 8 mph
b. 7 - 9 mph
c. 37 - 50 mph
d. 33 - 45 mph

# 6

# MANUAL TRANSMISSION AND REAR AXLE

STUDY OUTLINE

I.  Clutch Assembly

    A.  Components

        1.  Flywheel - purpose
        2.  Pilot bushing (bearing)
        3.  Friction disc, Torsional springs
        4.  Pressure plate
        5.  Clutch cover
        6.  Throwout bearing
        7.  Release levers

    B.  Adjustments and Linkage

        1.  Free-play clearance
        2.  Over-center spring

    C.  Problem/Diagnosis

        1.  Does not engage
        2.  Does not release
        3.  Noises

            a.  Pedal depressed
            b.  Pedal released

        4.  Pulsating pedal
        5.  Chatter
        6.  Slipping
        7.  Binding
        8.  Shudder in reverse

    D.  Replacement Procedures

        1.  Aligning mandrels
        2.  Guide pins

II. Manual Transmission

    A. Power Flow (3-speed and 4-speed)
    B. Components (Be Able To Identify Visually)

        1. Shafts
        2. Gears - nomenclature
        3. Bearings
        4. Thrust washers
        5. Synchromesh devices - operation
        6. Shift levers and linkage
        7. Interlock mechanism (detent)

    C. Rebuilding Procedures, Clearance Checks
    D. Problem/Diagnosis

        1. Noises
        2. Jumping out of gear
        3. Gears do not engage
        4. Backlash or end-play
        5. Stays locked in gear


III. Drive Line

    A. Type of Drive

        1. Hotchkiss
        2. Torque tube
        3. Four wheel

    B. Type of Universal Joints

        1. Cross/Yoke
        2. Constant velocity

            a. No speed fluctuation

        3. Service procedures

            a. Grease fitting direction

    C. Tube Design

        1. Tube-in-tube
        2. Solid
        3. Yokes

            a. Phasing

        4. Damper rings

D. Drive Shaft Alignment

    1. Companion flange run-out

E. Problem/Diagnosis

    1. Noise

        a. Acceleration rumble
        b. Deceleration clunk or rattle
        c. Squeaking

    2. Vibrations

        a. Changing drive line angle
        b. Checking balance with hose clamps

    3. Backlash (excessive play)

F. U-joint Wear Patterns

    1. Brinelling
    2. Trunion end-galling


IV. Differential and Axle Assembly

A. Types

    1. Full floating axles
    2. Semi floating axles
    3. Hypoid gear design
    4. Timed gear sets
    5. Trans-axle assemblies
    6. Gear ratio calculation

B. Construction and Components (Be Able To Identify Visually)

    1. Carrier and bearings
    2. Axle (side) gears
    3. Thrust washers
    4. Shafts
    5. Ring gear
    6. Drive pinion gear
    7. Drive pinion bearings
    8. Pinion (differential or "spider") gears
    9. Axle shaft and bearings

        a. End-play
        b. Removal

    10. Seals (direction of lip faces grease)

V.  Differential Service/Adjustments

A. Terms

   1. Preload
   2. Backlash
   3. Contact pattern (depth)

B. Drive Pinion Preload Adjustment

   1. Crush sleeve
   2. Shims

C. Drive Pinion Depth Setting

   1. Shims/Location
   2. Thickness and effect of change
   3. Depth markings

D. Carrier Bearing Preload

   1. Shims
   2. Threaded adjusters

E. Ring Gear Backlash

   1. Effect by movement of carrier
   2. Shims
   3. Threaded adjusters
   4. Specifications

F. Ring Gear Run-out
G. Differential Case Run-out
H. Tooth Contact Pattern

   1. Coast side
   2. Drive side
   3. Toe contact
   4. Heel contact
   5. Face contact
   6. Flank contact

I. Rebuilding Procedures

   1. Clearance checks
   2. Housing spreader

VI.  Problem/Diagnosis

   A. Noises

      1. Coast
      2. Drive
      3. Float

   B. On Turns
   C. Backlash Clunks
   D. Improper Lubricant (Limited Slip Differential)
   E. Limited Slip Differential Operational Test

---

EXERCISES

   1. A car is equipped with a standard transmission.  As the clutch
      pedal is pressed down, the clutch fork and bearing will contact the:

      a. Release levers
      b. Friction disc
      c. Clutch cover
      d. Pressure plate

   2. When the clutch pedal is pushed down (disengaged), the release
      levers:

      a. Do not contact the throwout bearings
      b. Release the pressure plate springs
      c. Pull the pressure plate back
      d. None of the above

   3. If a given tooth on the drive pinion gear matches with the same
      teeth on the ring gear during every revolution of the ring gear, the
      gear set is:

      a. Hunting
      b. Non-hunting
      c. Semi non-hunting
      d. Partial non-hunting

4. What is a hypoid gear set?


   a. Where the pinion engages the ring gear at the center line
   b. Where the pinion engages the ring gear below the center line
   c. Where the small end of the pinion is supported by a bearing
   d. Where a thrust block is used to control ring gear deflection


5. A 3-speed standard transmission is in low gear.  A 12-tooth main
   drive gear is meshed with a 30-tooth main drive cluster gear.  The
   cluster low gear has 14 teeth.  The low-reverse sliding gear has
   21 teeth.  What is the gear ratio in low?


   a. 2.5:1
   b. 3.75:1
   c. 4:1
   d. None of the above


6. A car is idling in the driveway.  The transmission is in neutral,
   and the clutch is engaged.  The cluster gear:


   a. Is not turning
   b. Is out of mesh with the main drive gear
   c. Lifts gear lubricant up to the mainshaft gears and bearings
   d. Does not run in the gear lubricant


7. A car owner complains of a chattering clutch.

   Mechanic A says that oil on the disc facing can be the problem.

   Mechanic B says that worn engine motor mounts can be the problem.

   Who is right?


   a. Mechanic A
   b. Mechanic B
   c. Either A or B
   d. Neither A nor B

8. What can cause a clutch to slip?

   a. Improper adjustment
   b. Oil soaked driven disc
   c. Weak pressure plate springs
   d. All of the above

9. What can cause a transmission to jump out of gear?

   a. Improper shift linkage adjustment
   b. Bell-housing misalingment
   c. Worn mainshaft bearings
   d. All of the above

10. The pilot bearing (or bushing) is located:

    a. On the rear of the output shaft
    b. On the main shaft
    c. Behind the main drive gear
    d. In the end of the crankshaft

11. Pilot or guide pins should be used in transmission installation
    to prevent damage to the:

    a. Clutch shaft
    b. Shift linkage
    c. Friction disc
    d. Main drive bearing

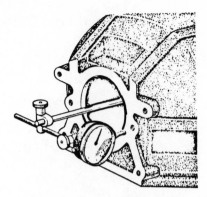

12. Bell-housing misalignment can cause a multitude of clutch and
    transmission problems.  When making the surface parallelism check
    shown above, the limit should be:


    a. .0015"
    b. .008"
    c. .060"
    d. .100"

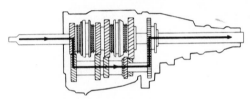

13. The above transmission is in what gear?


    a. First
    b. Second
    c. Third
    d. Reverse

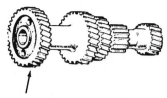

14. If several teeth were broken off the gear above (indicated by the arrow), the result would be noise in:

    a. First gear
    b. Second gear
    c. Reverse gear
    d. All of the above

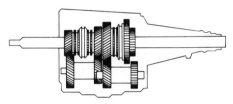

15. The above transmission is in what gear position?

    a. Neutral
    b. First
    c. Second
    d. Third

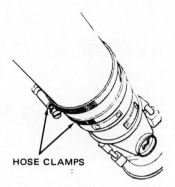

HOSE CLAMPS

16. What procedure is being performed on the above drive shaft?


    a. Balancing
    b. A run-out check
    c. An operating angle check
    d. Phase checking the yokes

17. The purpose of the above part is to permit the propeller shaft to:


    a. Change effective length
    b. Drive at an angle
    c. Slip during overload
    d. None of the above


18. When a car with a conventional differential makes a left turn:


    a. The left axle slows down.
    b. The right axle speeds up.
    c. Both axles receive the same torque.
    d. All of the above.

19. What is the ratio of a differential which has 39 teeth on the ring gear and 11 teeth on the drive pinion gear?

    a. 4.11 to 1 ratio
    b. 3.78 to 1 ratio
    c. 3.54 to 1 ratio
    d. None of the above

20. Mechanic A says that clutch cover bolts should always be released one at a time.

Mechanic B says that clutch cover bolts should be released evenly.

Who is right?

    a. Mechanic A
    b. Mechanic B
    c. Either A or B
    d. Neither A nor B

21. Brinelled wear spots on bearings and races generally indicate:

    a. Shock conditions or overloading
    b. High speed operation
    c. Lack of lubrication
    d. Improper installation

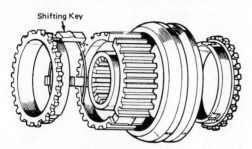

Shifting Key

22. In the illustration above, what is the purpose of the synchronizer shifting keys (inserts)?


a. To push the synchronizer ring against the gear cone
b. To prevent gear lock-up
c. To block the shift until speeds synchronize
d. To allow for gear disengagement


23. When the clutch is engaged, the friction disc is:


a. Not rotating
b. Pressed against the flywheel
c. Released from pressure plate tension
d. Both a and b

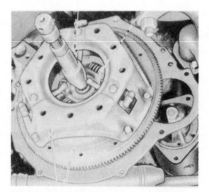

24. What procedure is being performed above?


a. Installing the pilot bearing
b. Removing the pilot bearing
c. Aligning the clutch disc
d. Setting release lever height

25. A broken right side engine mount could cause which of the following?


    a. A "shudder" in reverse
    b. A broken distributor cap
    c. A torn radiator hose
    d. All of the above

26. The above drive shaft has a heavy ring installed near the front.  This device acts to:


    a. Reduce vibration
    b. Dampen whirl noise
    c. Keep the joint velocity constant
    d. Control whip

27. What is the purpose of the above coil springs?


    a. To increase the force on the disc at high speeds
    b. To prevent clutch drag when shifting
    c. To dampen engine firing impulses from the drive line
    d. All of the above

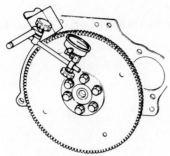

28. The above measurement check is not within specifications.  What
    could be the result?


    a. Shifts hard in all gears
    b. Jumps out of gear
    c. Pedal pulsation
    d. All of the above


29. You are installing a new flywheel ring gear that requires a shrink
    fit.  To avoid softening the gear teeth, do not heat above:


    a. 200°F
    b. 900°F
    c. 450°F
    d. 650°F

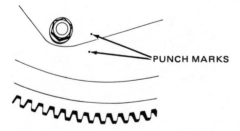

30. Why would a mechanic center punch mark the clutch cover and flywheel
    as shown above?


    a. To prevent cover warpage
    b. To maintain assembly balance
    c. To maintain correct release lever height
    d. All of the above

31. An engine has a noise similar to a main bearing knock.  A loose
    flywheel is suspected.

    Mechanic A says that one sure test for flywheel knock is to turn the
    ignition off, and then on, just as the engine is about to stop.

    Mechanic B says that flywheel knock will not generally change
    when the spark plugs are individually shorted out.

    Who is right?


    a. Mechanic A
    b. Mechanic B
    c. Both A and B
    d. Neither A nor B


32. The engine flywheel:


    a. Absorbs power (in effect) from the engine during the power stroke
    b. Is an inertia wheel
    c. Provides a mounting surface for the clutch cover
    d. All of the above

33. What part of the input shaft is the arrow above pointing to?


    a. Cone clutch surface
    b. Main drive gear
    c. Synchronizer hub
    d. Blocking ring

34. Mechanic A says that pedal free-play will increase as the friction disc wears.

    Mechanic B says that slippage can occur if pedal free-play is not correct.

    Who is right?

    a. Mechanic A
    b. Mechanic B
    c. Both A and B
    d. Neither A nor B

35. Mechanic A says that a slipping clutch can be caused by oil or grease on the facings.

    Mechanic B says that sticking or binding release levers can cause a clutch to slip.

    Who is right?

    a. Mechanic A
    b. Mechanic B
    c. Both A and B
    d. Neither A nor B

36. What could cause noise to come from the clutch bell-housing when the pedal is released?

    a. Frozen pilot bearing
    b. Loose friction disc hub
    c. Worn main drive gear bearing
    d. All of the above

37. A ball bearing is being inspected by spin testing.

    Mechanic A says to lightly lubricate the bearing raceways with oil after cleaning and drying.

    Mechanic B says to spin the outer bearing race using an air hose.

    Who is right?

    a. Mechanic A
    b. Mechanic B
    c. Both A and B
    d. Neither A nor B

38. A customer complains of vibration and chatter when the car is turning.

    Mechanic A says that in limited slip differentials, the wrong lubricant is a major cause.

    Mechanic B says that in conventional axles, too many differential pinion thrust washers can be the cause.

    Who is right?

    a. Mechanic A
    b. Mechanic B
    c. Both A and B
    d. Neither A nor B

39. Which of the following would most likely be a clutch pedal free-play adjustment specification?

    a. 1"
    b. 1/16"
    c. .030"
    d. 6"

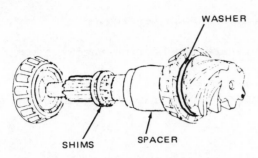

40. The drive pinion bearing preload is not enough on the differential
    unit that you are assembling.  Based on the illustration above,
    what needs to be done?


    a. Decrease the shim thickness.
    b. Increase the shim thickness.
    c. Remove the two shims and install an O/S spacer.
    d. Install the next thickness size washer.


41. A car is stationary, the engine is running, the 3-speed transmission
    is in neutral, and the clutch is engaged.  Which of the following
    gears are not turning?


    a. Countershaft gear (cluster)
    b. Reverse idler gear
    c. Second gear on mainshaft
    d. Sliding low and reverse


42. A differential makes noise on turns only.  You would strongly
    suspect:


    a. Worn drive pinion bearings
    b. Worn carrier bearings
    c. Worn differential pinion gears
    d. A defective axle bearing


43. As the clutch pedal is pressed down, the release levers will move
    the pressure plate away from the:


    a. Throwout bearing
    b. Clutch disc
    c. Clutch cover
    d. Apply springs

44. "Rear spring wrap-up" is a condition inherent to what type of vehicle?

    a. Torque tube drive
    b. Hotchkiss drive
    c. 4-wheel drive
    d. Front wheel drive

45. Semi-centrifugal clutch weights are generally located on the:

    a. Flywheel
    b. Pressure plate springs
    c. Clutch shaft
    d. Release levers

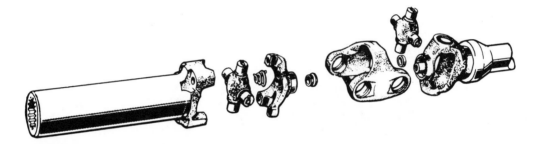

46. The above universal joint:

    a. Is a constant velocity u-joint
    b. Does not transfer motion at uniform speed
    c. Is a double Cardan u-joint
    d. Both a and c

47. A manual transmission slips out of high gear.  This can be caused by:

    a. The transmission loose on the bell-housing
    b. A worn countershaft
    c. Both a and b
    d. Neither a nor b

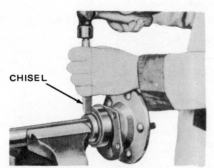

CHISEL

48. The mechanic above is:


   a. Removing the rear axle shaft grease seal
   b. Removing the wheel bearing retainer ring
   c. Safety staking the axle retainer
   d. Adjusting bearing preload


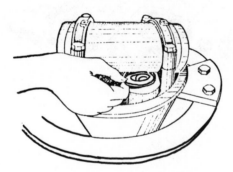

49. What check is being performed above?


   a. Housing distortion
   b. Crush sleeve size
   c. Pinion end-play
   d. Pinion depth

50. You are replacing a leaking pinion seal on a crush sleeve type differential.

    Mechanic A says that the entire rear axle assembly will have to be disassembled.

    Mechanic B says to make reference marks and tighten the pinion nut a slight additional amount.

    Who is right?


    a. Mechanic A
    b. Mechanic B
    c. Both A and B
    d. Neither A nor B

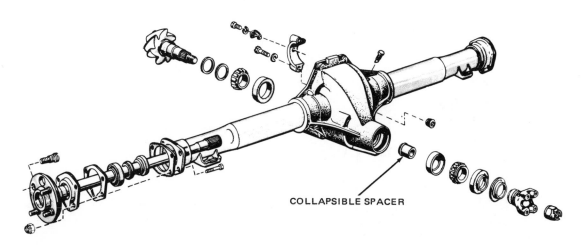

COLLAPSIBLE SPACER

51. Refer to the drawing above.

    Mechanic A says that the collapsible spacer prevents the forward pinion bearing cone from spinning on the drive pinion shaft.

    Mechanic B says that the spacer helps maintain pinion bearing preload.

    Who is right?


    a. Mechanic A
    b. Mechanic B
    c. Both A and B
    d. Neither A nor B

52. What is the "+2" marking on the above gear?

    a. Depth shim reference number
    b. Gear set number
    c. Preload setting number
    d. Backlash variance number

53. When measuring pinion bearing preload, which tool below is recommended?

    a. "Click" type torque wrench
    b. Dial type torque wrench
    c. Depth micrometer
    d. Dial indicator

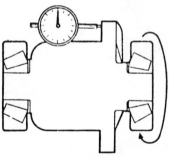

54. A differential assembly is being overhauled.  What would you consider
    to be the maximum allowable measurement (shown above)?

    a. .002"
    b. 1/64"
    c. .020"
    d. 1/32"

c  55. A car owner complains of vehicle vibration.  A check shows that
       the rear universal joint drive angle is not correct.

       Mechanic A says that sometimes this angle is changed by inserting a
       tapered wedge between the rear leaf springs and axle housing.

       Mechanic B says that on some vehicles the axle housing is tilted to
       provide the correct angle by adjusting the coil spring control arms.

       Who is right?


       a. Mechanic A
       b. Mechanic B
       c. Both A and B
       d. Neither A nor B

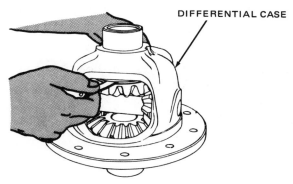

DIFFERENTIAL CASE

56. What is the mechanic above doing?


    a. Checking backlash between the side gear and the differential
       pinion shaft
    b. Checking clearance between the spider gear and the differential
       case
    c. Checking clearance between the side gear and thrust washer
    d. None of the above

57. Mechanic A says that an integral type (unitized) differential uses shims for adjusting backlash.

Mechanic B says that an integral type differential uses shims for adjusting carrier bearing preload.

Who is right?

a. Mechanic A
b. Mechanic B
c. Both A and B
d. Neither A nor B

58. What tool would you generally use to set carrier bearing preload on a rear axle assembly that uses nut locks (see above)?

a. Spanner wrench
b. Torque wrench
c. Spring scale
d. Dial indicator

59. What is the reason for having the drive pinion bearing properly preloaded?

Mechanic A says to prevent the pinion gear from moving away from the ring gear under load.

Mechanic B says to prevent bearing looseness under a driving situation.

Who is right?

a. Mechanic A
b. Mechanic B
c. Both A and B
d. Neither A nor B

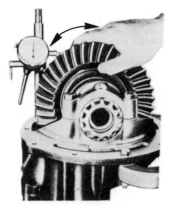

60. You are making the check shown above.

What figure would you consider to be acceptable?


    a. .0005" - .0015"
    b. .008" - .012"
    c. .030" - .040"
    d. .080" - .110"

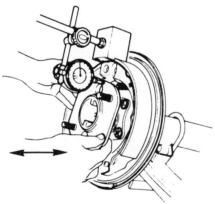

61. The item in the picture above is being moved back and forth.  What is the mechanic checking for?


    a. Axle end-play
    b. A warped flange
    c. A bad rear wheel bearing
    d. A bent axle

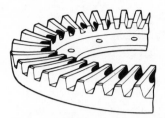

62. The above tooth pattern shows:


    a. Incorrect flank contact
    b. Incorrect toe contact
    c. Correct coast side contact
    d. None of the above

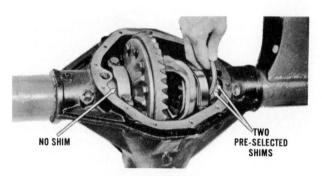

63. Refer to the picture above.  What will happen when two shims are removed from the right and shifted to the left side?


    a. Backlash will increase
    b. Backlash will decrease
    c. Preload will decrease
    d. None of the above

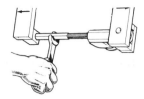

64. The above tool is used for:

   a. Spreading the differential housing
   b. Checking axle housing alignment
   c. Supporting the engine when the transmission is removed
   d. None of the above

65. When turning a corner, different rear axle speeds result.  What occurs in the differential to allow for this?

   a. The differential pinions turn on their own centers.
   b. The "spiders" are locked to the pinion shaft.
   c. The differential case is free-wheeling.
   d. One axle side gear is not turning.

AXLE SHAFT

C-LOCK

66. The c-lock shown above is taken out prior to:

   a. Axle shaft removal
   b. Removing the pinion shaft
   c. Both a and b
   d. Neither a nor b

67. Mechanic A says that speedometer error can result by changing rear tire size.

   Mechanic B says that speedometer error can result by changing rear axle gear ratio.

   Who is right?

   a. Mechanic A
   b. Mechanic B
   c. Both A and B
   d. Neither A nor B

68. Excessive counter gear (cluster) end-play can cause:

   a. Noise in all reduction gears
   b. Excessive backlash in all reduction gears
   c. Both a and b
   d. Neither a nor b

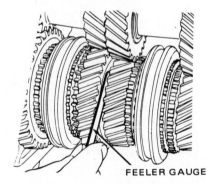

FEELER GAUGE

69. What check is being performed above?

   a. Synchronizer clearance
   b. Cluster lash
   c. Gear end-play
   d. None of the above

70. Direct drive (high gear) in a standard transmission is accomplished by:

    a. An idler gear
    b. A hub and sleeve assembly
    c. A cluster gear
    d. A countershaft

71. A clutch has a "squealing" noise when it is disengaged.  This is probably caused by:

    a. A damaged main drive gear
    b. Worn disc facing
    c. A worn release bearing
    d. The overcenter spring needing lubrication

72. The picture above shows:

    a. Installing the rear wheel bearing
    b. Installing the rear wheel bearing oil seal
    c. Removing the axle shaft
    d. None of the above

73. Drive line vibration on a vehicle with CV u-joints can be caused by:

    a. Worn center bearing support
    b. Bent centering ball stud
    c. Incorrect pinion flange angle
    d. All of the above

74. Parts of the clutch assembly that should not be washed in cleaning solvent are the:

    a. Friction disc and clutch cover
    b. Release levers and pressure plate
    c. Friction disc and throwout bearing
    d. Clutch cover and throwout bearing

75. The above arrow is pointing to the:


    a. Output shaft oil slinger
    b. Reverse idler gear
    c. Low and reverse gear
    d. Speedometer drive gear


76. Whenever replacing the drive pinion gear, always replace the:


    a. Differential pinion gears
    b. Side bearings
    c. Side gears
    d. Ring gear


77. A customer complains of a high-pitched "whine" noise similar to a whistle.  The noise occurs at all driving speeds and seems to come from the rear end of the vehicle.

    Mechanic A says the pinion bearings could be bad.

    Mechanic B says the differential may need lubricant.

    Who is right?


    a. Mechanic A
    b. Mechanic B
    c. Both A and B
    d. Neither A nor B

# 7

# ELECTRICAL SYSTEMS

STUDY OUTLINE

I.   Types of Circuits (Understand Voltage, Amperage, and Resistance
     Relationships in Each)

     A. Series
     B. Parallel
     C. Series Parallel


II.  Circuit Devices/Symbols

     A. Fuse
     B. Circuit Breaker
     C. Fusible Link
     D. Relays
     E. Switches
     F. Solenoids
     G. Diode
     H. Transistor
     I. Motors
     J. Lamps
     K. Resistor
     L. Ground
     M. Battery
     N. Connections (Male and Female)


III. Circuit Test Equipment and Hook-Up (Know How to Read the Different
     Scales on Meters)

     A. Voltmeter
     B. Ammeter
     C. Ohmmeter
     D. 12-volt Test Light
     E. Self-powered Test Light
     F. Short Detectors (Buzzers and Circuit Breakers)
     G. Jumper Wires

IV.  Circuit Testing (You Will be Asked to Use Schematics in Locating
     Diagnosis Test Points)

     A. Shorted Circuit
     B. Open Circuit
     C. Grounded Circuit
     D. Intermittent Circuit Problems


V.   Lighting Systems (Understand the Typical Operation for Each Circuit)

     A. Headlight Circuit

        1. High beam lamps
        2. Low beam lamps
        3. Dimmer switch
        4. Switch rheostat
        5. Wiring

     B. Stop Lamp Circuit
     C. Directional Signal Circuit

        1. Flasher types
        2. Switch replacement
        3. Flashing speed

     D. Hazard Warning Lights
     E. Tail Lamp Circuit
     F. Back-Up Lamp Circuit
     G. Instrument Panel and Interior Lights


VI.  Accessory Systems

     A. Basic Theory of Operation
     B. Basic Troubleshooting Procedures

        1. Oil sending unit
        2. Fuel gauge and tank sending unit
        3. Temperature warning
        4. Horns
        5. Constant voltage regulator for dash instruments

VII.  Battery

    A.  Safety Procedures
    B.  Open Flame and Explosion
    C.  Removal and Installation Procedure
    D.  Basic Construction and Chemical Action
    E.  Sizes and Ratings
    F.  Testing/Service

        1.  State of charge (hydrometer)
        2.  Cell voltage (light load test)
        3.  Capacity test
        4.  Sulfation (3-minute charge test)
        5.  Battery charging procedure
        6.  Cleaning
        7.  Jump starting

    G.  Interpretation of Test Results
    H.  Problem/Diagnosis

        1.  Corroded connections
        2.  Leakage (dirt on battery top)
        3.  No start complaints
        4.  Slow cranking complaints
        5.  Excessive water use
        6.  Discharges overnight (constant current drain)
        7.  Damaged plates

    I.  Storage

        1.  Dry charge
        2.  Wet charge
        3.  Slow charge


VIII.  Charging System

    A.  AC Type
    B.  DC Type
    C.  Advantages of the AC System
    D.  AC System Components Compared to DC System

        1.  Diodes/cut-out relay
        2.  Rotor/field
        3.  Stator/armature
        4.  Slip rings/commutator
        5.  Difference in amount of current carried by brushes
        6.  Residual magnetism

E. AC Charging Circuit Operation

   1. Schematic of Delco system (electro-mechanical)
   2. Schematic of Ford system (electro-mechanical)
   3. Voltage regulation
   4. Current control
   5. Light relay
   6. Field relay
   7. Ammeter circuit (instead of charge indicator light)

F. Test Equipment

   1. Voltmeter
   2. Ammeter
   3. Ohmmeter
   4. 1/4 ohm resistor
   5. Knife switch
   6. Diode testers
   7. Scope

G. Test Hook-Up/Interpretation of Results

   1. Field circuit (current draw)
   2. Rotor tests (shorts, grounds, continuity)
   3. Stator tests (shorts, grounds, continuity)
   4. Diode tests
   5. Output test
   6. Voltage regulator setting
   7. Insulated and ground circuit tests

H. Problem/Diagnosis

   1. Loose belts
   2. Open rotor circuit
   3. Grounded rotor circuit
   4. Defective diode(s)
   5. Noises

      a. Bearings
      b. Belts
      c. Mounting
      d. Stator
      e. Diode

   6. Defective Regulator

      a. "Full-field" Ford (A+ to F)
      b. "Full-field" Delco (F to 3)
      c. Fusible links
      d. Light relay
      e. Integral regulator

I. Alternator Rebuilding Procedures/Tools
J. Regulator Adjustments

IX. Starter (Cranking) System

A. Basic Function
B. Types and Basic Differences

    1. Delco
    2. Ford
    3. Chrysler

C. Construction and Nomenclature of Parts
D. Starter Drive Operation

    1. Bendix
    2. Overrunning clutch

E. Testing/Service

    1. Current draw using BST
    2. Field coil tests (shorts, grounds, continuity)
    3. Armature tests (shorts, grounds, continuity)

        a. Growler

    4. Insulated circuit voltmeter readings
    5. Ground circuit voltmeter readings

        a. Voltmeter readings

    6. Remote cranking Ford, G.M., and Chrysler systems
    7. Rebuilding procedures

        a. Undercutting mica
        b. Don't wash starter drive in solvent
        c. No-load test

F. Problem/Diagnosis

    1. Dragging armature
    2. Defective starter drive
    3. Worn bushings
    4. Worn flywheel ring gear
    5. Starter alignment (shims)
    6. Noise when cranking
    7. High current draw
    8. Low current draw
    9. Thrown armature windings

10. Will not crank
11. Cranks slowly
12. Burned commutator


X.  Starter Circuit Controls (Understand Basic Operation)

A. Relays

1. Ford system
2. Chrysler system

B. Solenoids

1. G.M. system
2. Ford system

C. Neutral Safety Switches
D. Resistor By-pass

1. G.M. system
2. Ford system
3. Chrysler system

E. Ignition Switches
F. Circuit Testing

1. Voltage drop readings
2. Solenoid tests

G. Problem/Diagnosis

1. "Chatter"
2. Ignition switch contact corrosion
3. Poor solenoid contact disc connection
4. Starter motor won't stop turning after ignition switch is
   placed in run position

EXERCISES

1. You are testing a cranking motor armature.  If a self-powered lamp
   lights when one test prod is placed on the armature core and the
   other prod is placed on the commutator bars, the armature is:

   a. Shorted
   b. Grounded
   c. Open circuited
   d. Testing normal

2. The brushes in an alternator carry:

   a. Field current
   b. Output current
   c. Voltage regulator current
   d. Both a and b above are correct.

3. The above electrical component is good.  When measuring this part
   with an ohmmeter and then measuring again with the leads reversed,
   you should have:

   a. Two low readings
   b. Two high (infinite) readings
   c. One high (infinite) and one low reading
   d. None of the above

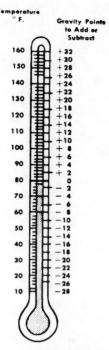

4. If a battery hydrometer reading is 1.280 and the electrolyte
   temperature reading is 50°F, the temperature corrected reading
   is (refer to the above conversion scale):


   a. 1.160
   b. 1.292
   c. 1.400
   d. 1.268


5. A late model automobile is towed into the repair shop.  The mechanic
   attempts to start the car.  The engine cranks very slowly and won't
   start.  Also, the headlights dim considerably during cranking.  What
   could be the problem?


   a. Worn starter brushes
   b. Shorted field windings in the starter
   c. High resistance in the insulated or ground circuit
   d. None of the above

6. Mechanic A says that the alternator cannot produce alternating
   current until the stator windings are energized by battery current.

   Mechanic B says that the alternator cannot produce alternating
   current until battery current flows through the field coils from
   the regulator.

   Who is right?

   a. Mechanic A
   b. Mechanic B
   c. Both A and B
   d. Neither A nor B

7. Which of the following is true of the overrunning clutch type
   starter drive?

   a. Uses a shift lever
   b. Will slip if the cranking load becomes too great
   c. Both a and b are correct.
   d. Neither a nor b

8. The alternator regulator controls output voltage by:

   a. Grounding the stator coils at the "Y" connection
   b. Grounding the diodes
   c. Grounding the field coil or by inserting resistance in the
      circuit feeding battery current to the field coil
   d. Grounding the rectifier bridge

9. A customer complains that the turn signals flash too slowly.
   This could be caused by:

   a. Wrong type of flasher
   b. Incorrect bulb wattage
   c. Both a and b
   d. Neither a nor b

10. Mechanic A says that a short circuit would result in increased current flow from the battery.

    Mechanic B says that a short circuit will cause a decrease in circuit resistance.

    Who is right?

    a. Mechanic A
    b. Mechanic B
    c. Both A and B
    d. Neither A nor B

11. You are going to make a battery capacity test on a battery.  The battery is marked only with the following information:
    Cold Cranking Current @ 0°F = 330
    Reserve Capacity (minutes) = 100

    What load should be applied with the BST carbon pile?

    a. 100 amps
    b. 115 amps
    c. 165 amps
    d. 50 amps

12. A field current draw test can be made on alternators (left mounted on the vehicle) to check for:

    a. A shorted rotor
    b. A grounded field coil
    c. Poor brush contact
    d. All of the above

13. A faulty DC generator regulator in which the cut-out relay points stay closed after the engine is stopped can cause:

    a. A dead battery
    b. Damaged generator windings
    c. A motoring generator
    d. All of the above

14. You are going to remove the battery from a negative ground system automobile and replace it with a new one.  Which of the following procedures is correct?

    a. Disconnect the ground cable first, and reconnect the positive cable first.
    b. Disconnect the ground cable first, and reconnect the positive cable last.
    c. Disconnect the positive cable first, and reconnect the ground cable first.
    d. Disconnect the positive cable first, and reconnect the ground cable last.

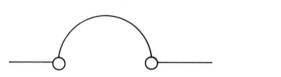 

15. The electrical symbols drawn above represent which of the following?

    a. Fuse and transistor
    b. Circuit breaker and diode
    c. Capacitor and transistor
    d. None of the above

16. Convert 35 milliamperes to amperes.  The answer would be:

    a. 35 amperes
    b. 3.5 amperes
    c. .35 amperes
    d. .035 amperes

17. Testing a storage battery using the above device will indicate:


    a. The overall battery condition
    b. The battery capacity
    c. The battery state of charge
    d. The battery voltage


18. You are going to make a high-rate discharge test on a 12-volt
    battery. The typical procedure calls for applying a load 3 times
    the ampere-hour rating, with the battery voltage falling:


    a. Not lower than 11 volts after 30 seconds
    b. Not lower than 9.6 volts after 15 seconds
    c. Not lower than 10.5 volts after 30 seconds
    d. Not lower than 6 volts after 15 seconds


19. The cutout relay is not required in the AC generator regulator
    because of the:


    a. Magnetic flux that is created
    b. Rotor windings
    c. Diodes
    d. Slip rings


20. The total current output of the alternator is limited by the:


    a. Field relay in the regulator
    b. Voltage limiter relay in the regulator
    c. Stator windings
    d. Diodes

21. Which of the following specific gravity readings would indicate a
    full state of charge (in a temperate climate)?

    a. 1.140
    b. 1.200
    c. 1.215
    d. None of the preceding

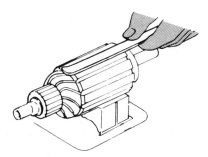

22. If the metal strip in the above picture vibrates, the armature is:

    a. Shorted
    b. Grounded
    c. Open circuited
    d. Testing normal

23. According to Ohm's Law:

    a. To find the amperage, multiply the voltage by the resistance.
    b. To find the voltage, divide the amperage by the resistance.
    c. To find the resistance, multiply the voltage by the amperage.
    d. None of the above are correct.

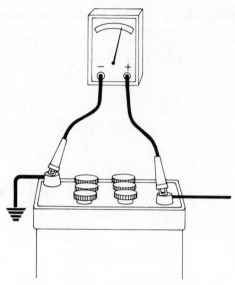

24. A voltmeter is connected across a 12V battery according to the above
    illustration.  A jumper lead is used to ground the ignition circuit
    to prevent the engine from starting.  With the ignition switch
    turned on and the engine cranking, the voltmeter should not read
    less than:


    a. 12.0 volts
    b. 10.5 volts
    c. 9.5 volts
    d. 7.5 volts


25. Which of the following items can cause an alternator to be noisy?
    1. Worn bearings  2. Loose alternator mounting  3. Loose pulley
    4. Defective diode


    a. "1" only
    b. "1" and "2" only
    c. "1," "2," and "3" only
    d. All of the above

26. You are testing an alternator with an oscilloscope. The above waveform pattern appears. What would this indicate?

    a. Normal condition
    b. Open diode
    c. Shorted diode
    d. Open stator

27. When soldering an electrical wiring connection, use:

    a. Acid core flux
    b. Rosin core flux
    c. Either a or b
    d. Neither a nor b

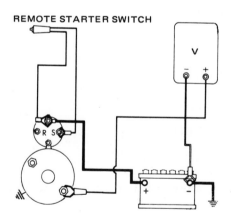

REMOTE STARTER SWITCH

28. A mechanic is performing a circuit resistance test according to the above diagram. The voltmeter reads 0.2 volt while the engine is being cranked. This indicates that:

    a. The ground circuit is satisfactory.
    b. The ground circuit has excessive resistance.
    c. The insulated circuit has excessive resistance.
    d. The positive battery cable should be replaced.

29. Alternator diodes are needed for:

    a. Controlling current output
    b. Rectification of AC current
    c. Rectification of DC current
    d. Protection against overcharging

30. When using an ammeter to perform a current draw test, a reading greater than specified would indicate:

    a. An open circuit
    b. Excessive circuit resistance
    c. A decrease in circuit resistance
    d. Either a or b above

31. Mechanic A says that in a discharged battery, most of the active material from the negative and positive plates has been converted to lead sulfate ($PbSO_4$), and the electrolyte is greatly diluted with water ($H_2O$).

    Mechanic B says that in a charged battery, the active material of the negative plate is sponge lead (Pb), the active material of the positive plate is lead peroxide ($PbO_2$), and the electrolyte contains sulfuric acid ($H_2SO_4$) with a minimum of water.

    Who is right?

    a. Mechanic A
    b. Mechanic B
    c. Both A and B
    d. Neither A nor B

32. Two lamps are wired in parallel.  If another lamp is added in parallel:

    a. The voltage will drop.
    b. The total current will decrease.
    c. The total resistance will increase.
    d. The total resistance will decrease.

33. Three lamps are wired in parallel.  What would happen if one lamp
    shorts out?

    a. The circuit amperage will decrease.
    b. The circuit resistance will increase.
    c. The other two lamps will stay on.
    d. The other two lamps will go out.

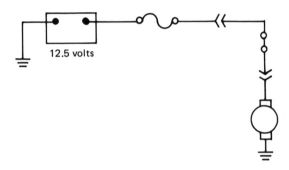

12.5 volts

34. The above windshield wiper motor has a 1.4 voltage drop in the
    power side of the circuit.  There is a 0.1 voltage drop in the
    grounded side.  How many volts are available to operate the motor?

    a. 11.0
    b. 11.1
    c. 12.4
    d. 12.5

35. A DC generator armature corresponds which part of the AC generator?

    a. Rotor
    b. Stator
    c. Diodes
    d. Slip rings

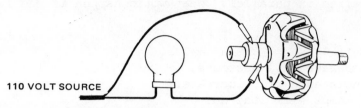

**110 VOLT SOURCE**

36. The test being performed above is a check for:

    a. Shorts
    b. Grounds
    c. Continuity
    d. High resistance

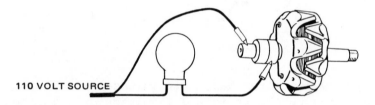

**110 VOLT SOURCE**

37. The test being performed above is a check for:

    a. Shorts
    b. Grounds
    c. Continuity
    d. High resistance

38. Mechanic A says that the ¼ ohm resistor setting on generator-alternator-regulator test machines is used to simulate a fully charged battery.

    Mechanic B says that the ¼ ohm resistor is used during voltage regulator testing.

    Who is right?

    a. Mechanic A
    b. Mechanic B
    c. Both A and B
    d. Neither A nor B

39. Battery electrolyte specific gravity should not vary more than _____ between cells.

    a. 0.10
    b. 0.50
    c. 0.050
    d. 0.005

40. Mechanic A says that when using an ohmmeter, a low or zero reading indicates continuity.

    Mechanic B says that a full-scale reading (infinity) indicates no continuity.

    Who is right?

    a. Mechanic A
    b. Mechanic B
    c. Both A and B
    d. Neither A nor B

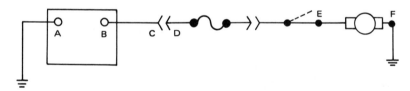

41. To measure current draw of the above motor, how would you connect an ammeter?

    a. Red to E, black to F
    b. Red to B, black to F
    c. Red to C, black to D
    d. Black to A, red to F

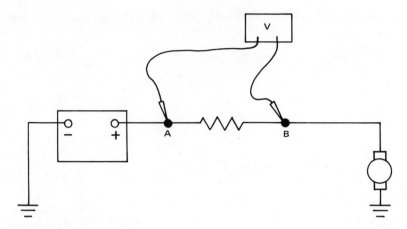

42. The voltmeter in the above hook-up reads zero volts. There is power to point A.

    Mechanic A says the resistor could be shorted.

    Mechanic B says that the circuit beyond point B could be open.

    Who is right?


    a. Mechanic A
    b. Mechanic B
    c. Both A and B
    d. Neither A nor B

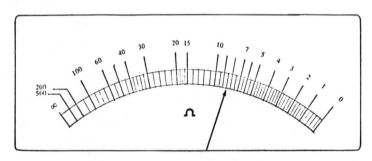

43. The above meter reading is:


    a. 8.5 ohms
    b. 85 ohms
    c. 850 ohms
    d. 8,500 ohms

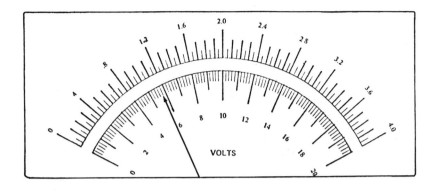

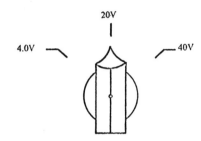

44. The above meter reading is:

    a. 4.9 volts
    b. 5.08 volts
    c. 5.4 volts
    d. 5.8 volts

45. A 12-volt battery (that just failed the capacity test) is being
    charged at 40 amps.  After 3 minutes of fast charge, with the charger
    still operating, a voltmeter hooked across the battery reads 15.8 volts.
    What is indicated?

    a. The battery should be slow charged and put back into service.
    b. Everything is normal.  Continue fast charge for a half hour,
       and put back into service.
    c. The battery is sulfated and should be replaced.
    d. The battery electrolyte should be replaced.

46. A battery is using excessive water.  This can be caused by:

    a. A high voltage regulator setting
    b. A shorted battery cell
    c. A poor regulator ground
    d. All of the above

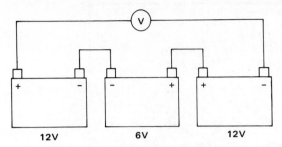

47. The above voltmeter will show a reading of:


    a. 6 volts
    b. 12 volts
    c. 18 volts
    d. 24 volts


48. The low beam headlamps do not light.  The problem is more than likely in the:


    a. Dimmer switch
    b. Headlamp
    c. Thermal circuit breaker
    d. Common socket ground

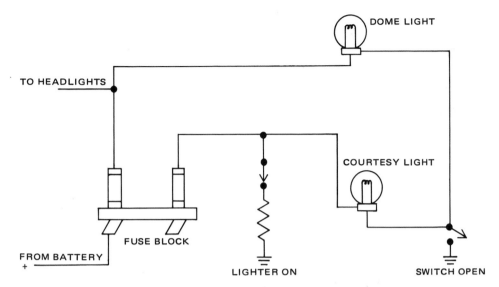

49. A customer complains that the cigarette lighter in his car doesn't pop out. Also, when the lighter is depressed, the dome light and courtesy light glow. According to the above diagram, what could be wrong?


    a. A poor lighter ground
    b. A blown lighter fuse
    c. Low circuit resistance
    d. A burned out lighter element


50. Mechanic A says that whenever a DC generator has been disconnected, repaired or replaced, it must be polarized before being put back into operation.

    Mechanic B says that it is unnecessary to polarize an AC generator and may result in serious regulator damage if attempted.

    Who is right?


    a. Mechanic A
    b. Mechanic B
    c. Both A and B
    d. Neither A nor B

51. A customer complains that the left front directional light doesn't
    work.  The left rear, right front, and right rear directional
    lights work.  The most likely cause would be a:

    a. Faulty flasher
    b. Defective directional switch
    c. Burned out bulb
    d. Shorted wire

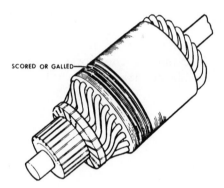

SCORED OR GALLED

52. The above condition could be caused by:

    a. Worn bearings
    b. Loose pole shoe
    c. Bent armature shaft
    d. All of the above

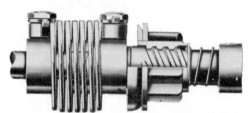

53. On the above type of starter motor drive, how is the pinion gear
    engaged with the flywheel ring gear?

    a. By the anti-drift spring
    b. Through a shift lever
    c. By reason of pinion inertia
    d. By the drive spring

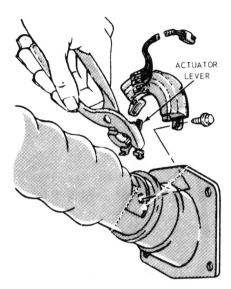

54. Mechanic A says that if the above switch and actuator are not
    installed correctly, the starter control circuit won't operate
    properly.

    Mechanic B says that the back-up lights won't work properly.

    Who is right?


    a. Mechanic A
    b. Mechanic B
    c. Both A and B
    d. Neither A nor B

55. What is the purpose of the small hole in the ignition switch shown above?

   Mechanic A says that this hole is used when releasing the lock cylinder from the switch.

   Mechanic B says that this hole is used for periodic lubrication of the tumbler mechanism.

   Who is right?


   a. Mechanic A
   b. Mechanic B
   c. Both A and B
   d. Neither A nor B

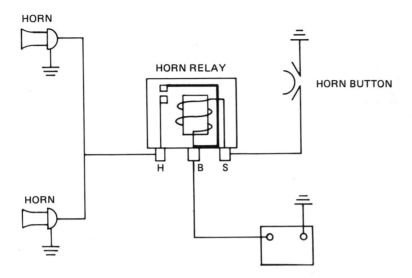

56. A customer complains that the horn doesn't honk. When wire B above is disconnected at the horn relay and touched to the H terminal connection, the horn honks.

    Mechanic A says that the horn button mechanism could be defective.

    Mechanic B says that the horn relay could be defective.

    Who is right?

    a. Mechanic A
    b. Mechanic B
    c. Both A and B
    d. Neither A nor B

57. Which of the following is true?

    I.  A horn relay keeps current flow through the steering wheel contacts at a minimum.

    II. Many horn relays use a shunt resistor to eliminate the possibility of the driver getting an induced electric shock when honking the horn.

    a. I only
    b. II only
    c. Both I and II
    d. Neither I nor II

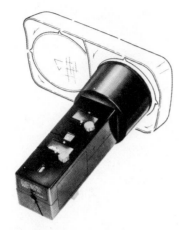

58. Mechanic A says that the headlamps have to be turned on when using
    the above aimer.

    Mechanic B says that the car must be on a perfectly level surface
    when using the above aimer.

    Who is right?


    a. Mechanic A
    b. Mechanic B
    c. Both A and B
    d. Neither A nor B

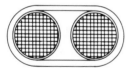                                    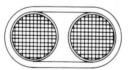

59. In the dual headlighting system shown above:


    a. Both outside lamps are double filament low and high beam.
    b. Both outside lamps are double filament high beam only.
    c. Both inside lamps are double filament low and high beam.
    d. Both inside lamps are double filament high beam only.

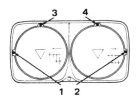

60. Pictured above is a left front dual headlamp assembly.  When making the vertical aim adjustment for the low beam lamp, which adjusting screw would you turn?


    a. 1
    b. 2
    c. 3
    d. 4

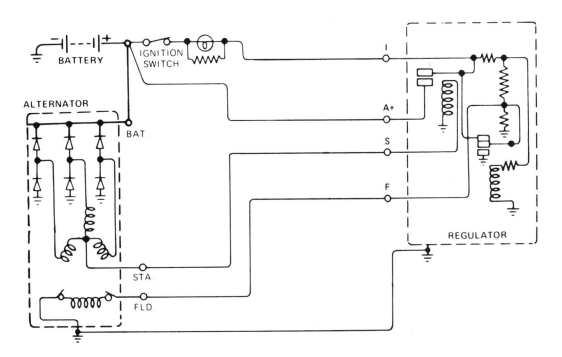

61. To "full-field" the above alternator, disconnect the regulator multiple connector plug and:


    a. Connect a jumper between A+ and S on the regulator.
    b. Connect a jumper from A+ to S in the connector.
    c. Connect a jumper from A+ to F on the regulator.
    d. Connect a jumper from A+ to F in the connector.

62. Refer to the schematic for question #61.  If this regulator was
    used with an ammeter, which terminal would not be necessary?

    a. I
    b. A+
    c. S
    d. F

63. Refer to the schematic for question #61.  If an electric carburetor
    choke was wired into the circuit, where would the connection be?

    a. At the alternator FLD terminal
    b. At the alternator STA terminal
    c. At the alternator BAT terminal
    d. At the regulator A+ terminal

64. Refer to the schematic for question #61.  Where would an ammeter be
    placed in the circuit for an output check?

    a. In series with the alternator STA terminal
    b. In series with the alternator FLD terminal
    c. In parallel with the alternator BAT terminal
    d. In series with the alternator BAT terminal

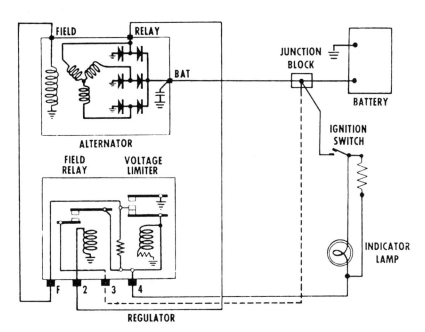

65. Mechanic A says to "full-field" the above alternator, you would take
a jumper wire and ground the F terminal at the alternator.

Mechanic B says that you would disconnect the multiple connector at
the regulator and connect a jumper wire from F to 4 in the connector.

Who is right?

a. Mechanic A
b. Mechanic B
c. Both A and B
d. Neither A nor B

66. In the schematic for question #65, the indicator lamp will light
when the ignition switch is turned on. Where does this lamp obtain
its ground?

a. In the voltage regulator
b. In the field coil
c. In the field relay
d. At the alternator BAT terminal

67. How is a DC voltmeter usually connected when making electrical checks?

    a. Across a circuit
    b. In parallel
    c. In series
    d. Both a and b above

68. The maximum current output of an alternator is limited by the:

    a. Stator CEMF
    b. Regulator
    c. Battery capacity
    d. Diode size

69. When soldering alternator diode connections, why are long noise pliers often used to hold the diode leads?

    a. The pliers act as a heat sink.
    b. To prevent overheating the stator windings
    c. To prevent stator core damage
    d. To prevent end frame heat sink damage

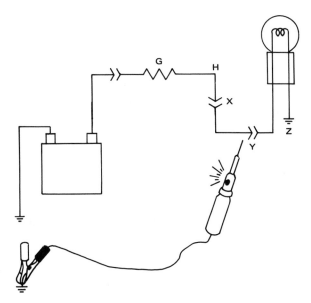

70. The above test light does not light when the point is placed at Y.
    It lights when placed at H or X.  The defect is:


    a. Resistor G is open
    b. Bad ground at Z
    c. Wire XY is open
    d. Bulb is burned out

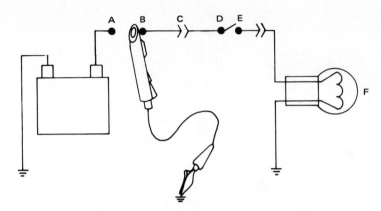

71. A self-powered test light has been connected to point B as shown
    above.  The light glows with bulb F disconnected and continues to
    glow as switch DE is opened.  The light goes out when C is separated.
    What is indicated?

    a. Switch DE is shorted to ground.
    b. Wire CD is shorted to ground.
    c. The circuit is testing okay.
    d. Wire CD is open.

72. A starter motor amperage draw test is being performed.  An unusually
    low reading is indicated (accompanied by a slow cranking speed).

    Mechanic A says that a possible cause could be poor brush or commutator
    condition.

    Mechanic B says that the armature rubbing on the pole shoes could be a
    possible cause.

    Who is right?

    a. Mechanic A
    b. Mechanic B
    c. Both A and B
    d. Neither A nor B

73. The basic purpose of an overrunning clutch in the starter drive is to:

    a. Assist the solenoid during cranking
    b. Pull the starter pinion gear out of mesh
    c. Disengage the armature when the engine starts
    d. Keep the hold-in winding energized during cranking

74. What occurs when two adjacent conductors make electrical contact and by-pass a portion of the circuit?

    a. A ground
    b. An open
    c. A short
    d. Circuit resistance increases

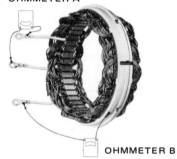

OHMMETER A

OHMMETER B

75. Mechanic A says that ohmmeter A above is making a check for an open, and ohmmeter B is checking for a short.

    Mechanic B says that ohmmeter A is testing for a ground, and ohmmeter B is testing for an open.

    Who is right?

    a. Mechanic A
    b. Mechanic B
    c. Both A and B
    d. Neither A nor B

76. In a series circuit:


    a. The current is the same throughout the entire circuit.
    b. There is a voltage drop across each resistance.
    c. The sum of all the voltage drops is equal to the source voltage.
    d. All of the above are correct.


77. In a parallel circuit:


    a. The voltage is the same throughout the circuit, but the current
       is divided.
    b. The total circuit resistance is always smaller than the smallest
       resistor in the circuit.
    c. There is more than one path for the current to flow.
    d. All of the above are correct.

"R" TERMINAL

78. The above solenoid has an "R" terminal that is used to:


    a. Supply current directly to the ignition coil
    b. Supply current to the ignition resistor
    c. Activate the pull-in winding
    d. Activate the hold-in winding

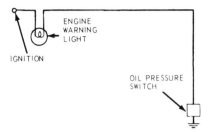

79. The above red warning light "flickers" on and off when the car is driven down the road.

    Mechanic A says that the wire could have come off at the pressure switch and is intermittently grounding.

    Mechanic B says that the engine could be low on oil.

    Who is right?


    a. Mechanic A
    b. Mechanic B
    c. Both A and B
    d. Neither A nor B


80. Mechanic A says that a "chattering" starter solenoid plunger can be caused by an open circuited hold-in winding.

    Mechanic B says that the pull in winding could be open circuited.

    Who is right?


    a. Mechanic A
    b. Mechanic B
    c. Both A and B
    d. Neither A nor B


81. The red charge indicator light fails to light with the ignition switch turned to the RUN position with the engine stopped. What could be the problem?


    a. This condition is normal on most cars.
    b. The bulb is burned out.
    c. The field relay is failing to close.
    d. Either b or c above

82. Both turn signals work, but will not cancel.  What could be the
    cause?

    a. Wrong wattage flasher
    b. Steering wheel installed 180° out of correct position
    c. Defective turn signal switch
    d. Either b or c above

83. The hazard warning lights will not flash.  The turn signals function
    normally.

    Mechanic A says that the hazard warning buzzer could be inoperative.

    Mechanic B says that the turn signal switch could be defective.

    Who is right?

    a. Mechanic A
    b. Mechanic B
    c. Both A and B
    d. Neither A nor B

84. Mechanic A says that a battery is likely to freeze during cold
    weather if it has a high specific gravity.

    Mechanic B says that a battery is likely to freeze with a low state
    of charge.

    Who is right?

    a. Mechanic A
    b. Mechanic B
    c. Both A and B
    d. Neither A nor B

85. Electrical accessories on cars are protected against short circuits by:

    a. Fusible links
    b. Circuit breakers
    c. Fuses
    d. All of the above

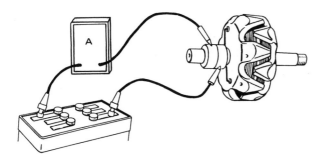

86. The above test is generally made when testing for a:


    a. Shorted circuit
    b. Grounded circuit
    c. High resistance circuit
    d. Open circuit

87. If the above alternator component is shorted, it will cause:


    a. Radio noise
    b. Battery drain
    c. Lower current output
    d. All of the above

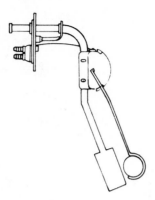

88. The above item has been removed from the vehicle.  What would you
    use to accurately check it?


    a. An ohmmeter
    b. A self-powered test light
    c. A shunt wound ammeter
    d. A voltmeter

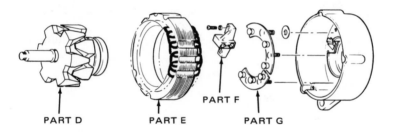

89. In the above alternator assembly, where are the diodes located?


    a. Part D
    b. Part E
    c. Part F
    d. Part G

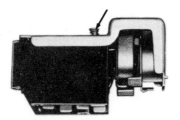

90. What is the arrow pointing to on the headlight switch shown above?


    a. Circuit breaker reset button
    b. Knob release button
    c. Rheostat adjustment
    d. Dashboard light override

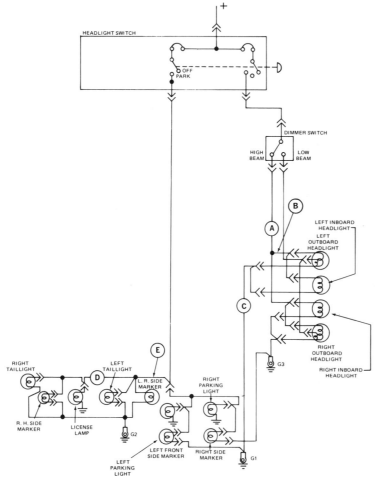

91. If the tail lights and rear side marker lights fail to operate in
    the above circuit, but the license plate light does, the most
    likely cause is:


    a. Wire E open
    b. Wire D open
    c. Ground wire G2 missing
    d. Ground wire G4 missing

92. Refer to the circuit diagram for question #91.  The left inboard
and left outboard high beam filaments do not work.  Both right
side high beam filaments operate.  Both low beams are okay.  What
could be wrong?


a. Wire A open
b. Wire B open
c. Wire C open
d. Ground wire G3 missing

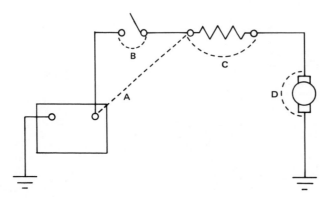

93. You are using a jumper wire to by-pass parts in the above circuit.
Which jumper is being used according to general recommended
procedure?

a. A only
b. B only
c. A and B only
d. B, C, and D only


94. What is the possible result from a too tight alternator drive belt?

Mechanic A says the belt will become glazed.

Mechanic B says that alternator front bearing failure can result.

Who is right?


a. Mechanic A
b. Mechanic B
c. Both A and B
d. Neither A nor B

95. Where do you find the IC alternator regulator mounted?


    a. On the firewall
    b. On the fender apron
    c. Under the dash
    d. Attached to the alternator


96. What happens to the field relay contact points when the engine is
    started in a system that has a charge indicator light?

    Mechanic A says that they open.

    Mechanic B says that they close.

    Who is right?


    a. Mechanic A
    b. Mechanic B
    c. Both A and B
    d. Neither A nor B


97. A car is factory equipped with separate oil and temperature gauges.
    The temperature gauge only reads improperly.

    Mechanic A says that the instrument voltage regulator could be the
    trouble.

    Mechanic B says that the trouble may be in the printed circuit board.

    Who is right?


    a. Mechanic A
    b. Mechanic B
    c. Both A and B
    d. Neither A nor B


98. The word "shunt" describes a type of _____ circuit.


    a. Open
    b. Series
    c. Parallel
    d. Ground

# 8

# HEATING AND AIR CONDITIONING

STUDY OUTLINE

I. Air Conditioning System

    A. Basic Principles of Refrigeration

        1. Temperature/Pressure relationship

    B. System Components, Purpose, and Operation of Each

        1. Evaporator
        2. Compressor
        3. Condenser
        4. Receiver-drier

            a. Fusible safety plug

        5. Expansion valve

            a. Sensing bulb

    C. Refrigerant Flow
    D. Types of Systems (Temperature Controls)

        1. Cycling
        2. STV
        3. POA
        4. EPR
        5. VIR
        6. Manual and vacuum controls (blend type)

    E. High and Low Side
    F. "Touch" Test
    G. Condition of R-12 at Various Circuit Points

II. System Service

    A. Manifold Gauge Set

        1. Hose hook-up

            a. Attachment with third gauge

        2. Hand valve positions
        3. Normal gauge readings

    B. Service Valves

        1. Schrader connections

    C. Safety in Handling of R-12

        1. Storage
        2. Discharging

    D. Evacuation Procedure
    E. Isolation of Compressor
    F. Checking Compressor Oil
    G. Charging Procedure

        1. Adding refrigerant as a liquid
        2. Charging with vapor

    H. Leak Testing

        1. Halide
        2. Electronic
        3. Soap
        4. Dytel

    I. Flushing Contaminated System
    J. Valve Plates
    K. Seal Replacement

III.  Problem/Diagnosis

    A. Engine Overheating
    B. Noisy System Operation

        1. Mounts
        2. Bearings (pulley/clutch)
        3. Belts
        4. Excessive high or low charge
        5. Moisture in the refrigerant

    C. Insufficient Cooling
    D. Intermittent Cooling
    E. No Cooling at All
    F. Windshield Fogging
    G. Abnormal Low Side Readings

H. Abnormal High Side Readings
I. Frost on Evaporator
J. Sight Glass

    1. Clear
    2. Foam (bubbles)
    3. Oily

K. Electrical Circuit Problems

    1. Blown fuse
    2. Defective wiring
    3. Bad connections
    4. Defective thermostat
    5. Magnetic clutch

L. Effects of Moisture in System
M. POA Systems Pressures
N. EPR Systems Pressures
O. Air Distribution

    1. Vacuum motors
    2. Manual cables
    3. Blower motor

        a. Relays
        b. Fuses
        c. Resistors

IV. Heating Systems

A. Components

    1. Blend doors
    2. Blower switch
    3. Control valves
    4. Plenum chamber

B. Flow Control Valve Operation

    1. "Bowden" cable operated
    2. "Ranco" valve
    3. Restricted heater (touch)
    4. Small hose usually inlet

C. Thermostat (Function)

D. Service

   1. Electrolysis damage
   2. "Block-Check" test
   3. Testing radiator pressure cap
   4. Reverse flushing
   5. Fluid fan inspection

E. Problem/Diagnosis

   1. No heat
   2. Too much heat (cannot control)

F. Blower Motors

   1. Ducting - AC/heating
   2. Heater core position
   3. Evaporator position

---

EXERCISES

1. When a can of R-12 refrigerant is released to the atmosphere (at sea level), it starts to "boil" rapidly at a temperature of:

   a. -80°F
   b. -22°F
   c. -0°F
   d. 212°F

2. In an air conditioning system the refrigerant is a _____ as it leaves the compressor.

   a. Low pressure gas
   b. High pressure liquid
   c. High pressure gas
   d. Low pressure liquid

3. The condenser:

   a. Changes high pressure vapor into low pressure liquid
   b. Changes high pressure vapor into high pressure liquid
   c. Changes low pressure vapor into low pressure liquid
   d. Changes high pressure liquid into low pressure liquid

4. The refrigerant line leading from the evaporator to the compressor contains:

    a. Low pressure gas
    b. Low pressure liquid
    c. High pressure gas
    d. High pressure liquid

5. In normal operation, the line mentioned in question #4 should feel:

    a. Cold to the touch
    b. Hot to the touch
    c. Extremely hot to the touch
    d. Extremely cold to the touch

6. What will the halide leak detector flame color be when a large refrigerant leak is present?

    a. Red
    b. Yellow-green
    c. Blue-green
    d. Pale blue

7. Mechanic A says that "add-on" air conditioning units use a Robotrol valve.

    Mechanic B says that a Selectrol valve is used.

    Who is right?

    a. Mechanic A
    b. Mechanic B
    c. Both A and B
    d. Neither A nor B

8. If R-12 comes into contact with a flame:

    a. It will explode.
    b. It will turn to a non-toxic gas.
    c. Iodine crystals are formed.
    d. Phosgene gas will form.

9. Any storage container or air conditioning system containing liquid R-12 (at rest and subject to an ambient temperature of 70°F) will have an internal pressure of approximately:

    a. 220 psi
    b. 125 psi
    c. 70 psi
    d. 30 psi

10. Mechanic A says to never steam clean near the components or lines of an air conditioning system because the heat can cause excessive pressure build-up.

Mechanic B says to never discharge R-12 into a closed area, because it is heavier than air and can displace the air you breathe.

Who is right?

    a. Mechanic A
    b. Mechanic B
    c. Both A and B
    d. Neither A nor B

11. Which a/c components separate the high pressure side from the low pressure side?

    a. Evaporator and condenser
    b. Condenser and expansion valve
    c. Compressor and expansion valve
    d. Evaporator and condener

12. Of the following readings, which is closest to a normal low side operating gauge pressure?

    a. 5-10 psi
    b. 15-30 psi
    c. 35-50 psi
    d. 180-205 psi

13. When evacuating an a/c system, the manifold gauge hand valves are in which position?

    a. Both sides closed
    b. Both sides open
    c. Low side open, high side closed
    d. Low side closed, high side open

| EVAPORATOR PRESSURE GAUGE READING P.S.I. | EVAPORATOR TEMPERATURE °F | HIGH PRESSURE GAUGE READING P.S.I. | AMBIENT TEMPERATURE °F |
|---|---|---|---|
| 0 | -21 | 72 | 40 |
| 4.5 | -10 | 105 | 60 |
| 11.2 | 4 | 113 | 64 |
| 13.4 | 8 | 122 | 68 |
| 15.8 | 12 | 129 | 71 |
| 18.3 | 16 | 134 | 73 |
| 21 | 20 | 140 | 75 |

14. According to the above chart, if the temperature of the outside air reaching a normal working air conditioner is 71°F, the pressure in the discharge side of the system is:

    a. 129 psi
    b. 15.8 psi
    c. 12 psi
    d. None of the above

15. Excessive moisture in an air conditioning system will cause freezing at the:

    a. Receiver-drier
    b. Evaporator
    c. Thermostatic expansion valve
    d. Compressor

16. A car owner says that his air conditioner is not properly cooling.

    Mechanic A says that an overcharge of R-12 could be the cause.

    Mechanic B says that the heater water valve could be the cause.

    Who is right?


    a. Mechanic A
    b. Mechanic B
    c. Both A and B
    d. Neither A nor B


17. The low pressure gauge reads 20" Hg after 15 minutes of evacuation.
    This would indicate:

    a. Further evacuation needed
    b. Evacuation is completed
    c. A large leak in the system
    d. A normal condition


18. A mechanic discovers that an air conditioning system has way too
    much "head pressure."  The most likely cause of this problem is:


    a. Condenser clogged by bugs, lint, etc.
    b. Leaking thermal bulb
    c. Open by-pass valve
    d. Malfunctioning thermostatic switch


19. Moisture contamination in the refrigeration system can cause:


    a. Corrosion, rust, and sludge
    b. Hydrochloric and hydrofluoric acid
    c. Ice
    d. All of the above

a 20. An air conditioning unit (switch de-icing type) freezes the coils regardless of temperature control setting.

Mechanic A says that a seized clutch bearing could be the problem.

Mechanic B says that moisture in the system could be the problem.

Who is right?

a. Mechanic A
b. Mechanic B
c. Both A and B
d. Neither A nor B

b 21. Mechanic A says that when installing the receiver-drier, be sure the arrow points away from the evaporator.

Mechanic B says the receiver-drier should be installed as nearly vertical as possible.

Who is right?

a. Mechanic A
b. Mechanic B
c. Both A and B
d. Neither A nor B

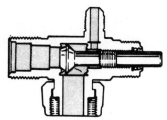

a 22. What is the position of the above service valve?

a. Front seated
b. Back seated
c. Mid position
d. Normal operating position

23. Mechanic A says that if refrigerant will not enter the system due
    to low temperature, place the R-12 container in 125°F hot water.

    Mechanic B says to warm up the R-12 container with a propane torch.

    Who is right?

    a. Mechanic A
    b. Mechanic B
    c. Either A or B
    d. Neither A nor B

24. Mechanic A says that no bubbles in the sight glass could indicate too
    much refrigerant.

    Mechanic B says that no bubbles could indicate a complete loss of
    refrigerant.

    Who is right?

    a. Mechanic A
    b. Mechanic B
    c. Either A or B
    d. Neither A nor B

25. A heater core has just been boiled out.  The car owner still complains
    of insufficient heat.

    Mechanic A says that the trouble could be an improperly functioning
    blend door.

    Mechanic B says that a defective thermostat could be the trouble.

    Who is right?

    a. Mechanic A
    b. Mechanic B
    c. Either A or B
    d. Neither A nor B

26. When evacuating an air conditioning system, which manifold gauge hose is connected to the vacuum pump?

   a. High pressure hose
   b. Low pressure hose
   c. Center hose
   d. Either a or b above

27. Air conditioning system pressures vary with:

   a. Humidity
   b. Altitude
   c. Temperature
   d. All of the above

28. Mechanic A says that when servicing a system with the above type of service valve, the compressor can't be isolated.

   Mechanic B says that the above valve permits a direct reading of the suction and discharge lines without having to manually front seat or back seat.

   Who is right?

   a. Mechanic A
   b. Mechanic B
   c. Both A and B
   d. Neither A nor B

29. The valve pictured in question #28 is known as a:

    a. POA valve
    b. Hot gas by-pass valve
    c. Schrader valve
    d. EPR valve

30. You are testing an air conditioning system with an EPR valve.

    Mechanic A says that the high side gauge reading should fall within the normal range of 90-110 psi.

    Mechanic B says that 140-210 psi would be correct.

    Who is right?

    a. Mechanic A
    b. Mechanic B
    c. Either A or B
    d. Neither A nor B

31. Mechanic A says that windshield fogging can be caused by a plugged evaporator drain.

    Mechanic B says that a leaking heater core can be the cause.

    Who is right?

    a. Mechanic A
    b. Mechanic B
    c. Both A and B
    d. Neither A nor B

32. On a cycling clutch air conditioning system, the low pressure gauge reading is high. The high pressure gauge reads low.

   Mechanic A says that an expansion valve stuck open could be the cause.

   Mechanic B says that a restricted receiver-drier could be the cause.

   Who is right?

   a. Mechanic A
   b. Mechanic B
   c. Both A and B
   d. Neither A nor B

33. On a cycling clutch air conditioning system the low pressure gauge reading is low. The high pressure gauge reads low also.

   Mechanic A says that o-ring leakage is a probable cause.

   Mechanic B says that the expansion valve bulb might be located in the wrong place.

   Who is right?

   a. Mechanic A
   b. Mechanic B
   c. Both A and B
   d. Neither A nor B

34. Mechanic A says that the high side gauge will read in the lower normal range with high ambient temperature.

   Mechanic B says that the high side gauge will read in the upper normal range with low ambient temperature.

   Who is right?

   a. Mechanic A
   b. Mechanic B
   c. Both A and B
   d. Neither A nor B

35. On a cycling clutch air conditioning system, the low side reading is normal. The high side reading is too low.

    Mechanic A says that compressor internal leakage is indicated.

    Mechanic B says that an overcharge of refrigerant oil is a possible cause.

    Who is right?

    a. Mechanic A
    b. Mechanic B
    c. Both A and B
    d. Neither A nor B

36. "Purging" a system too fast will result in:

    a. Forming phosgene gas
    b. Pulling oil from the compressor
    c. Reed valve damage
    d. Suction accumulator damage

37. You are performing a system evacuation. The vacuum pump should be operated a minimum of _____ upon reaching 29" Hg.

    a. 5 minutes
    b. 15 minutes
    c. 30 minutes
    d. 45 minutes

38. Temperature of stored R-12 must never exceed:

    a. 40°F
    b. 72°F
    c. 90°F
    d. 120°F

39. An air conditioning system is contaminated with metal particles.

    Mechanic A says to flush the system using distilled water.

    Mechanic B says to flush the system using dry nitrogen.

    Who is right?

    a. Mechanic A
    b. Mechanic B
    c. Either A or B
    d. Neither A nor B


40. STV, POA, ETR, and EPR valves are designed to:

    a. Control evaporator temperature
    b. Control condenser pressure
    c. Control compressor pressure
    d. Both a and c above are correct


41. Mechanic A says that the suction throttling valve (STV) can be cable controlled.

    Mechanic B says that it is adjustable.

    Who is right?

    a. Mechanic A
    b. Mechanic B
    c. Both A and B
    d. Neither A nor B


42. A THIRD gauge is often used in combination with a conventional high and low pressure manifold gauge set.  This THIRD gauge permits the mechanic to:

    a. Compare the THIRD gauge reading with the low side gauge reading.
    b. Compare the THIRD gauge reading with the high side gauge reading.
    c. Compare the THIRD gauge reading with figures listed in the pressure/ temperature relationship chart.
    d. Compare the THIRD gauge reading with discharge air temperature at the evaporator outlet register.

43. Mechanic A says that a suction throttling valve not regulating properly could cause insufficient air flow from the instrument panel registers.

    Mechanic B says that a suction throttling valve not regulating properly could cause the evaporator to ice up.

    Who is right?

    a. Mechanic A
    b. Mechanic B
    c. Both A and B
    d. Neither A nor B

44. An air conditioning system is equipped with an EPR valve. When a THIRD gauge is connected into the compressor service port, it will read:

    a. Line pressure
    b. Compressor high side pressure
    c. Discharge pressure
    d. Suction pressure

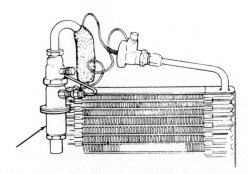

45. The arrow in the above picture is pointing to:

    a. An expansion valve
    b. An EPR valve
    c. A VIR valve
    d. None of the above

46. Mechanic A says that a defective POA valve can cause evaporator pressure to be either too high or too low.

    Mechanic B says that adjustment is possible on POA valves.

    Who is right?


    a. Mechanic A
    b. Mechanic B
    c. Both A and B
    d. Neither A nor B


47. You observe a slight seepage of compressor oil from the compressor shaft seal.  This condition is:


    a. Normal
    b. A sign that the seal requires immediate replacement
    c. An indication that the compressor shaft surface is damaged
    d. Either b or c above

48. How would you check oil level in the above compressor?


    a. By draining the oil
    b. With an oil inducer tool
    c. With a special dipstick
    d. With a pressure gauge

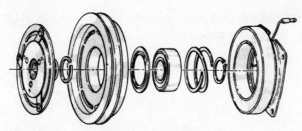

49. Refer to the above exploded-view illustration.

    Mechanic A says that slight scoring of the drive plate is a normal
    condition.

    Mechanic B says that slight scoring of the driven plate is a normal
    condition.

    Who is right?


    a. Mechanic A
    b. Mechanic B
    c. Both A and B
    d. Neither A nor B


50. An extremely noisy compressor would most likely be caused by:


    a. Clutch wire shorted
    b. High head pressures
    c. Slipping compressor clutch
    d. Defective ambient cut-off switch

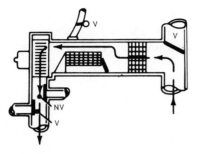

51. Refer to the above heater-air conditioning system illustration.
Which dash control setting would provide the air flow as shown?


    a. Recirculate a/c position
    b. Fresh a/c position
    c. Defrost position
    d. Maximum heat position

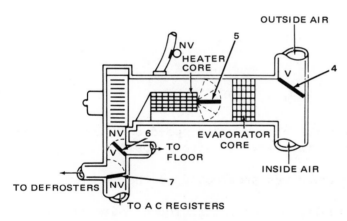

52. Refer to the above heater-air conditioning system illustration.
When the air conditioner is turned on, there is no cool air flowing
from the a/c registers. However, cool air flows out of the defroster
outlets. Which vacuum door is not operating?


    a. 4
    b. 5
    c. 6
    d. 7

53. Refer to the illustration for question #52.  In either the high or low heat position, there is no heat to the floor.  However, warm air flows from the defrosters.  Which vacuum door is not working properly?

    a. 4
    b. 5
    c. 6
    d. None of the above

54. When performing cooling system service, air can become trapped in the heater core.

    Mechanic A says to bleed the trapped air from the heater core outlet hose.

    Mechanic B says to bleed the trapped air by turning the heater on.

    Who is right?

    a. Mechanic A
    b. Mechanic B
    c. Either A or B
    d. Neither A nor B

55. A customer complains that the blower motor speed does not increase when the selector is moved from low to defrost position.

    Mechanic A says that a blower resistor could be the problem.

    Mechanic B says that a faulty blower motor ground could be the problem.

    Who is right?

    a. Mechanic A
    b. Mechanic B
    c. Both A and B
    d. Neither A nor B

56. When both manual service valves are in the back-seated position:

    a. The compressor is isolated.
    b. Service procedures can be performed.
    c. The suction side and discharge side of the compressor are
       cut off.
    d. The compressor is in normal operating position.

57. The outlet heater hose that leads to the water pump has been
    removed.  The engine is started, and the heater control switch
    is turned on.  The heater core outlet shows no water flow.

    Mechanic A says that the heater core could be plugged.

    Mechanic B says that the heater water valve could be defective.

    Who is right?

    a. Mechanic A
    b. Mechanic B
    c. Both A and B
    d. Neither A nor B

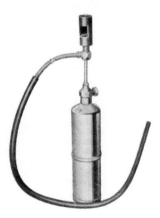

58. Mechanic A says that when using the above torch, keep the flame
    as small as possible.

    Mechanic B says that the copper element must be red hot.

    Who is right?

    a. Mechanic A
    b. Mechanic B
    c. Both A and B
    d. Neither A nor B

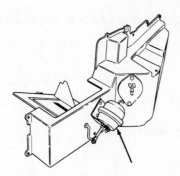

59. The arrow in the above illustration is pointing to a:

    a. Vacuum door motor
    b. Water valve
    c. Vacuum supply tank
    d. Plenum chamber

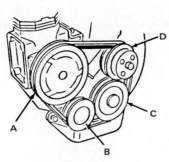

60. When replacing the above compressor drive belt, at which pulley
    would the tension most likely be adjusted?

    a. Pulley A
    b. Pulley B
    c. Pulley C
    d. Pulley D

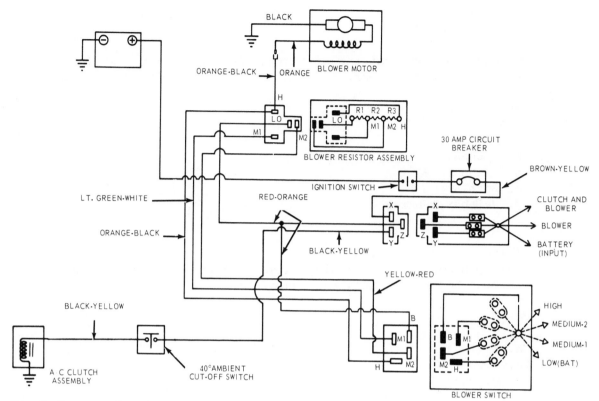

61. Refer to the above electrical circuit diagram. When the blower
    switch is in the MEDIUM-2 speed position, how many resistors are
    in the circuit to control blower motor speed?


    a. 3
    b. 2
    c. 1
    d. 0


62. Refer to the diagram for question #61. What would prevent the a/c
    clutch from engaging?

    Mechanic A says that the 30-amp circuit breaker could be defective.

    Mechanic B says that the red-orange wire could be open.

    Who is right?


    a. Mechanic A
    b. Mechanic B
    c. Both A and B
    d. Neither A nor B

63. Mechanic A says that the discharge side hose is smaller than the suction side hose.

    Mechanic B says that the discharge side hose should be cool when given the "touch" test.

    Who is right?

    a. Mechanic A
    b. Mechanic B
    c. Both A and B
    d. Neither A nor B

64. Which of the following figures would best represent the size of the opening in the expansion valve that the R-12 has to pass through before entering the evaporator?

    a. 1/4"
    b. 1/8"
    c. 0.008"
    d. 0.0005"

65. With the air conditioning system operating, insert a thermometer into the evaporator with the tip touching the coil. The temperature should be around:

    a. 35°F
    b. 55°F
    c. 72°F
    d. None of the above

66. A manifold gauge set has been hooked up to the suction and discharge sides of the compressor.  The center hose has been blocked off.

    Mechanic A says that system pressure is read when the gauge hand valves are open.

    Mechanic B says that system pressure is read when the gauge hand valves are closed.

    Who is right?

    a. Mechanic A
    b. Mechanic B
    c. Both A and B
    d. Neither A nor B

67. Clutch bearing failure noise would be:

    a. Much less when the compressor is engaged
    b. Much worse when the compressor is engaged
    c. The same whether or not the compressor is engaged
    d. Only heard when the compressor is engaged

68. An air conditioning system is being charged with vapor.  Which of the following is correct?

    a. Close the high-side hand valve.
    b. Open the low-side hand valve.
    c. Hold the refrigerant drum upright.
    d. All of the above

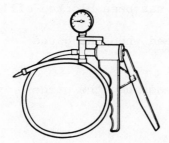

69. You are testing a blend door vacuum motor using the above tool.
    You connect the tool into the line going to the motor, and obtain
    a zero vacuum reading.  This would indicate:

    a. The door is restricted.
    b. The line to the motor is plugged or kinked.
    c. The vacuum motor is defective.
    d. Any of the above

70. Which of the following statements is correct?

    a. Refrigerant gas is heavier than air and will rapidly drop to
       the floor as it flows from a point of leakage.
    b. The total refrigerant charge circulates through the entire
       system at least once each minute.
    c. Just one drop of water added to the refrigerant system can
       result in corrosion.
    d. All of the above

71. Which of the following leak detection methods indicates a leak
    by a red-colored stain?

    a. Halide
    b. Dytel
    d. Flame
    d. Electronic

72. A heater core is rust-corroded and needs flushing.

    Mechanic A says to clean the core by high pressure reverse flushing.

    Mechanic B says to clean the core by flushing with a gentle water stream.

    Who is right?

    a. Mechanic A
    b. Mechanic B
    c. Either A or B
    d. Neither A nor B

73. You are recharging an air conditioning system. The refrigerant is being added as a liquid. Which of the following is correct?

    a. Tip the refrigerant can upside-down.
    b. Open the low-side hand valve.
    c. Open the high-side hand valve and run the engine.
    d. None of the above

74. When "touching" the inlet and outlet of the receiver-drier, the temperature:

    a. Should feel warm at the inlet and cold at the outlet
    b. Should feel cold at the inlet and warm at the outlet
    c. Should feel almost identical at the inlet and outlet
    d. Should feel warm at the inlet and hot at the outlet

75. A six-cylinder compressor is being rebuilt. When installing the ceramic seal, what procedure is correct?

    a. Coat the seal seat face with clean compressor oil.
    b. Depress the seal seat retainer ring into position by tapping it with a hammer.
    c. Both a and b
    d. Neither a nor b

76. What is the mechanic doing in the picture above?


    a. Removing the front discharge valve plate assembly
    b. Removing the suction reed plate
    c. Removing the rear discharge valve plate assembly
    d. None of the above

77. The two-cylinder compressor part shown above is a:


    a. Cylinder head
    b. Wobble plate
    c. Valve plate
    d. Suction crossover cover


78. A mechanic is hooking up a manifold gauge set that has color-coded
    hoses.  The blue hose is connected to:


    a. Vacuum
    b. Refrigerant
    c. The low side
    d. The high side

# ANSWERS

CHAPTER 1 - BRAKES

| | | | | | | | |
|---|---|---|---|---|---|---|---|
| 1- b | 12- d | 23- a | 34- d | 45- b | 56- d | 66- a | 77- a |
| 2- a | 13- a | 24- d | 35- d | 46- c | 57- c | 67- a | 78- c |
| 3- a | 14- d | 25- b | 36- b | 47- d | 58- b | 68- b | |
| 4- c | 15- b | 26- c | 37- b | 48- c | 59- b | 69- c | |
| 5- d | 16- c | 27- a | 38- d | 49- c | 60- b | 70- a | |
| 6- b | 17- c | 28- a | 39- c | 50- d | 61- b | 71- c | |
| 7- b | 18- b | 29- b | 40- d | 51- b | 62- c | 72- c | |
| 8- a | 19- a | 30- b | 41- a | 52- b | 63- b | 73- b | |
| 9- a | 20- d | 31- b | 42- c | 53- d | 64- d | 74- a | |
| 10- b | 21- d | 32- d | 43- c | 54- d | 65- a | 75- d | |
| 11- b | 22- c | 33- c | 44- b | 55- b | | 76- b | |

CHAPTER 2 - FRONT ENDS

| | | | | | | | |
|---|---|---|---|---|---|---|---|
| 1- a | 12- c | 23- b | 34- a | 45- c | 56- b | 67- b | 78- d |
| 2- a | 13- a | 24- b | 35- b | 46- d | 57- a | 68- c | 79- d |
| 3- d | 14- c | 25- c | 36- d | 47- c | 58- a | 69- a | 80- c |
| 4- b | 15- c | 26- b | 37- c | 48- b | 59- c | 70- c | 81- d |
| 5- a | 16- d | 27- a | 38- c | 49- c | 60- c | 71- a | 82- c |
| 6- b | 17- b | 28- b | 39- c | 50- b | 61- c | 72- d | |
| 7- b | 18- c | 29- c | 40- d | 51- d | 62- a | 73- c | |
| 8- c | 19- c | 30- a | 41- c | 52- c | 63- d | 74- c | |
| 9- a | 20- a | 31- c | 42- c | 53- a | 64- a | 75- c | |
| 10- c | 21- b | 32- c | 43- d | 54- c | 65- a | 76- d | |
| 11- a | 22- c | 33- c | 44- a | 55- b | 66- c | 77- c | |

CHAPTER 3 - ENGINE REPAIR

| | | | | | | |
|---|---|---|---|---|---|---|
| 1- b | 12- b | 23- b | 34- b | 45- a | 56- a | 67- c |
| 2- c | 13- c | 24- c | 35- d | 46- a | 57- b | 68- b |
| 3- b | 14- a | 25- d | 36- a | 47- c | 58- d | 69- c |
| 4- c | 15- c | 26- b | 37- a | 48- b | 59- d | 70- c |
| 5- c | 16- b | 27- b | 38- c | 49- d | 60- d | 71- a |
| 6- c | 17- c | 28- b | 39- c | 50- c | 61- b | 72- c |
| 7- b | 18- a | 29- d | 40- a | 51- d | 62- d | 73- c |
| 8- c | 19- b | 30- c | 41- b | 52- c | 63- c | 74- a |
| 9- b | 20- d | 31- a | 42- d | 53- b | 64- b | 75- c |
| 10- d | 21- a | 32- d | 43- d | 54- c | 65- c | 76- d |
| 11- b | 22- a | 33- d | 44- c | 55- b | 66- a | |

CHAPTER 4 - ENGINE TUNE-UP

| | | | | | | | |
|---|---|---|---|---|---|---|---|
| 1- d | 15- b | 29- a | 43- b | 57- d | 71- c | 85- b | 99- c |
| 2- b | 16- b | 30- d | 44- d | 58- a | 72- c | 86- b | 100-a |
| 3- d | 17- a | 31- b | 45- c | 59- c | 73- d | 87- c | 101-c |
| 4- c | 18- b | 32- b | 46- c | 60- a | 74- d | 88- d | 102-c |
| 5- b | 19- a | 33- c | 47- c | 61- c | 75- c | 89- c | 103-d |
| 6- c | 20- c | 34- c | 48- c | 62- c | 76- a | 90- c | 104-b |
| 7- a | 21- d | 35- d | 49- d | 63- b | 77- b | 91- c | 105-a |
| 8- a | 22- b | 36- a | 50- d | 64- c | 78- c | 92- b | 106-c |
| 9- b | 23- c | 37- b | 51- b | 65- c | 79- a | 93- b | 107-a |
| 10- c | 24- b | 38- c | 52- a | 66- c | 80- b | 94- a | 108-b |
| 11- a | 25- c | 39- a | 53- b | 67- b | 81- b | 95- b | 109-d |
| 12- d | 26- c | 40- a | 54- d | 68- c | 82- d | 96- c | 110-c |
| 13- b | 27- a | 41- a | 55- c | 69- b | 83- c | 97- a | 111-d |
| 14- b | 28- c | 42- d | 56- b | 70- d | 84- c | 98- a | |

## CHAPTER 5 - AUTOMATIC TRANSMISSIONS

| | | | | | | | |
|---|---|---|---|---|---|---|---|
| 1- b | 11- c | 21- c | 31- d | 41- d | 51- a | 61- d | 71- b |
| 2- c | 12- d | 22- c | 32- b | 42- b | 52- c | 62- a | |
| 3- c | 13- a | 23- c | 33- c | 43- c | 53- b | 63- a | |
| 4- c | 14- b | 24- b | 34- a | 44- c | 54- c | 64- b | |
| 5- c | 15- d | 25- d | 35- c | 45- a | 55- b | 65- c | |
| 6- a | 16- c | 26- a | 36- a | 46- d | 56- c | 66- b | |
| 7- d | 17- c | 27- d | 37- d | 47- a | 57- c | 67- b | |
| 8- a | 18- a | 28- d | 38- c | 48- a | 58- c | 68- d | |
| 9- d | 19- d | 29- d | 39- c | 49- c | 59- d | 69- a | |
| 10- c | 20- d | 30- b | 40- d | 50- c | 60- a | 70- c | |

## CHAPTER 6 - MANUAL TRANSMISSION AND REAR AXLE

| | | | | | | |
|---|---|---|---|---|---|---|
| 1- a | 11- c | 22- a | 33- a | 44- b | 55- c | 66- a |
| 2- c | 12- b | 23- b | 34- b | 45- d | 56- c | 67- c |
| 3- b | 13- d | 24- c | 35- c | 46- d | 57- c | 68- c |
| 4- b | 14- d | 25- d | 36- d | 47- a | 58- a | 69- c |
| 5- b | 15- a | 26- a | 37- a | 48- b | 59- c | 70- b |
| 6- c | 16- a | 27- c | 38- c | 49- d | 60- b | 71- c |
| 7- c | 17- a | 28- d | 39- a | 50- b | 61- a | 72- c |
| 8- d | 18- d | 29- c | 40- a | 51- c | 62- b | 73- d |
| 9- d | 19- c | 30- b | 41- d | 52- a | 63- b | 74- c |
| 10- d | 20- b | 31- c | 42- c | 53- b | 64- a | 75- d |
| | 21- a | 32- d | 43- b | 54- a | 65- a | 76- d |
| | | | | | | 77- c |

## CHAPTER 7 - ELECTRICAL SYSTEMS

| | | | | | | | |
|---|---|---|---|---|---|---|---|
| 1- b | 14- a | 27- b | 40- c | 53- c | 66- b | 79- c | 92- b |
| 2- a | 15- d | 28- a | 41- c | 54- c | 67- d | 80- a | 93- c |
| 3- c | 16- d | 29- b | 42- c | 55- a | 68- a | 81- b | 94- b |
| 4- d | 17- c | 30- c | 43- c | 56- c | 69- a | 82- d | 95- d |
| 5- b | 18- b | 31- c | 44- d | 57- c | 70- c | 83- c | 96- b |
| 6- b | 19- c | 32- c | 45- c | 58- d | 71- b | 84- b | 97- b |
| 7- a | 20- c | 33- d | 46- d | 59- a | 72- a | 85- d | 98- c |
| 8- c | 21- d | 34- a | 47- c | 60- d | 73- c | 86- a | |
| 9- c | 22- a | 35- b | 48- a | 61- d | 74- c | 87- d | |
| 10- c | 23- d | 36- c | 49- b | 62- a | 75- d | 88- a | |
| 11- c | 24- c | 37- b | 50- c | 63- b | 76- d | 89- d | |
| 12- d | 25- d | 38- c | 51- c | 64- d | 77- d | 90- b | |
| 13- d | 26- c | 39- c | 52- d | 65- d | 78- a | 91- c | |

## CHAPTER 8 - HEATING AND AIR CONDITIONING

| | | | | | | | |
|---|---|---|---|---|---|---|---|
| 1- b | 12- b | 23- a | 34- d | 45- d | 56- d | 67- a | 78- c |
| 2- c | 13- b | 24- c | 35- a | 46- a | 57- c | 68- d | |
| 3- b | 14- a | 25- c | 36- b | 47- a | 58- c | 69- c | |
| 4- a | 15- c | 26- c | 37- c | 48- c | 59- a | 70- d | |
| 5- a | 16- c | 27- d | 38- d | 49- c | 60- b | 71- b | |
| 6- c | 17- a | 28- c | 39- b | 50- b | 61- c | 72- b | |
| 7- c | 18- a | 29- c | 40- a | 51- a | 62- a | 73- a | |
| 8- d | 19- d | 30- b | 41- c | 52- d | 63- a | 74- c | |
| 9- c | 20- a | 31- c | 42- a | 53- c | 64- c | 75- a | |
| 10- c | 21- b | 32- a | 43- c | 54- c | 65- a | 76- c | |
| 11- c | 22- a | 33- a | 44- d | 55- a | 66- c | 77- c | |

# BIBLIOGRAPHY

Abbott, Sheldon L. *Automotive Brakes*. Beverly Hills, Calif.: Benziger, Bruce & Glencoe, 1977.

Abbott, Sheldon L. and Hinnerman, Ivan D. *Automotive Suspension and Steering*. Beverly Hills, Calif.: Benziger, Bruce & Glencoe, 1976.

*A.E.A. Technical Training Manuals*. Detroit, Mich.: Automotive Electrical Association.

*Ammco Brake Service Manual*. Detroit, Mich.: Marshalls, Inc.

*Automotive Service Guides*. Chicago, Ill.: Check-Chart Corporation.

*Automatic Transmission Service Guide*. Newark, N.J.: Lincoln Technical Institute.

Bacon, E. Miles *Principles of Wheel Alinement Service,* 2nd ed. New York, N.Y.: McGraw-Hill, 1977.

*Barrett Brake Training Manual*. Lansing, Mich.: John Bean Division, FMC Corporation.

Crouse, William H. and Anglin, Donald L. *Automotive Air Conditioning*. New York, N.Y.: McGraw-Hill, 1977.

Crouse, William H. *Automotive Electrical Equipment,* 7th ed. New York, N.Y.: McGraw-Hill, 1971.

Crouse, William H. and Anglin, Donald L. *Automotive Emission Control,* 2nd ed. New York, N.Y.: McGraw-Hill, 1977.

Crouse, William H. and Anglin, Donald L. *Automotive Engines,* 5th ed. New York, N.Y.: McGraw-Hill, 1976.

Crouse, William H. *Automotive Mechanics,* 7th ed. New York, N.Y.: McGraw-Hill, 1975.

Crouse, William H. and Anglin, Donald L. *Automotive Transmissions and Power Trains*. New York, N.Y.: McGraw-Hill, 1976.

*Delco-Remy Electrical Training Manuals*. Anderson, Ind.: Delco-Remy Division of General Motors Corporation.

Dwiggins, Boyce H. *Automotive Air Conditioning*. Albany, N.Y.: Delmar Publishers, 1969.

Dwiggins, Boyce H. *Automotive Steering Systems*. Albany, N.Y.: Delmar Publishers, 1969.

Ellinger, Herbert E. *Automechanics*. Englewood Cliffs, N.J.: Prentice-Hall, 1972.

*Hot Rod Magazine Technical Library Series Books*. Los Angeles, Calif.: Peterson Publishing Co.

*The How and Why of Automotive Lubrication Service*. Chicago, Ill.: Check-Chart Corporation.

*The How and Why of Automotive Tune-up Service*. Chicago, Ill.: Check-Chart Corporation.

*The How and Why of Tire, Battery, and Accessory Service*. Chicago, Ill.: Check-Chart Corporation.

*IMI Emission Control & Tune-up Manual*. Evanston, Ill.: Ignition Manufacturers Institute, 1969.

Johnson, James A. *Automotive Diagnosis and Tuneup*, 2nd ed. New York, N.Y.: McGraw-Hill, 1977.

*Motor Magazine*. New York, N.Y.: Hearst Publications.

Stockel, Martin W. *Auto Service and Repair*. Homewood, Ill.: Goodheart-Willcox, 1969.

*TBA Service Manuals*. Detroit, Mich.: United Motors Service Division of General Motors Corporation.

Toboldt, William K. and Purvis, Jud. *Motor Service's Automotive Encyclopedia*. Homewood, Ill.: Goodheart-Willcox Co., 1962.

Venk, Ernest A. and Billiet, Walter E. *Automotive Fundamentals,* 2nd ed. Chicago, Ill.: American Technical Society, 1962.

*Wagner Hydraulic Brake Service Manual*. St. Louis, Mo.: Parts and Accessories Division of Wagner Electric Corporation.

Webster, Jay *Principles of Automatic Transmissions*. Ann Arbor, Mich.: Prakken Publications, 1974.

Wetzel, Guy *Automotive Tune-up and Diagnosis*. Milpitas, Calif.: Master Technical Press, 1972.

# INDEX

4 ~

*Index*

8806